Your Sabbath Invitation

YOUR SABBATH INVITATION

Partnership in God's Ultimate Celebration

David R. Nekrutman

Your Sabbath Invitation

ISBN 978-0-578-26251-2 • FIRST EDITION

Copyeditor
Pamela Idriss

Graphic Designer
Samir Idriss

Printed and bound in the United States of America

I dedicate this book to my mother Natalie, my brother Joseph, my wife Kalanit, to my sons Jonathan, Ori, and Ariel, and to the memory of my father Allen. The book is also dedicated to Rabbi Dr. Gerald Meister of blessed memory because he was the Divine agent God used to direct me into the sacred calling of Jewish-Christian relations.

Contents

Tables and Figures

Number	Description	Page

Tables

Figures

Acknowledgements

Words cannot express my deep appreciation for Emilie and Craig Wierda, Dr. Brad Young and Dr. Gayle Young, Pamela and Samir Idriss, Terry and Robbie Mason, Sherry and Randy Lush, Janet Cain, Dr. Mark Rutland, Dr. Thomson Mathew, Dr. Cheryl Iverson, Dr. Glenda and Brad Payas, Gary and Connie Bachman, Dr. LaSalle and Portia Vaughn, the New Life Christian Center family, and New Life Christian Academy Hybrid. I am tremendously grateful to Rabbi Shlomo Riskin, Pastor Adam and Melanie Thornton, Omer Toledano, Pastor Mark Biltz, Dr. Victoria and Paul Sarvadi, Dr. Bron Barkley, the Greenlee family, Priscilla Flory, Karen and Joe Thompson, Helene B. Jones, and to Dr. Nancy Cook and her enthusiastic students.

Preface

In all honesty, my original intention was to write a book on the Hebraic roots of the Holy Spirit, but God had other plans. You see, I am the first Orthodox Jew to graduate with a master's degree from a Spirit-filled Christian university. I attended the College of Theology and Ministry at Oral Roberts University (ORU) in Tulsa, Oklahoma and earned a Master of Arts in Biblical Literature with a Concentration in Judaic-Christian Studies. My master's thesis investigated the concept of "הֶסְתֵּר פָּנִים" (*Hester Panim*, Hide Face) and its intricate relationship with the Holy Spirit, as manifested in God's *Shekinah*. The examination required interactions with Deuteronomy 31:16–18, the Book of Esther, and numerous ancient and modern rabbinical writings. A *Hester Panim* is a state of "Divine concealment," where God superficially "hides His face" from His people (Israel) during times of tragedy, disobedience, ethical sins, and idolatry. From *our human* perspective, God's face is supposedly concealed, but the "concealment" has a greater purpose from *His Divine* perspective. So, a key objective in my thesis was to understand how to access God during a *Hester Panim*–especially in the darkest of times–in order to 1) ascertain His greater purpose; 2) accomplish His purpose; and 3) end the Divine concealment.

Studying the *Hester Panim* in the Book of Esther was a compelling task. While God's Divine name is never stated in Esther, His name "יְהוָה," "The Eternal" (Author's translation), appears almost twenty times in Deuteronomy 31. The *Hester Panim* in Esther also meets the "tragedy" aspect of Divine concealment because Israel was facing complete annihilation. In the final chapter of the thesis, I demonstrated and concluded that *Hester Panim* is not so much a description of a *hidden* God as it is a depiction of The Eternal One *in hiding*, waiting for humanity to remove Him out of exile–beginning with the time of the destruction of the Second Temple through the present day. Ultimately, the thesis satisfied my intentions and provided practical applications for today.

Understanding *Hester Panim* within Deuteronomy 31 and the Book of Esther now offers invaluable help and hope for the contemporary tragedies Israel has faced. Additionally, my exploration revealed ways believers can access God during His concealment and simultaneously acquire a deeper and more meaningful relationship with Him, via His Holy Spirit expressed through the *Shekinah.*

The master's thesis was the most challenging writing project I had ever encountered! After graduating in 2018, I was relieved, elated, and suddenly motivated

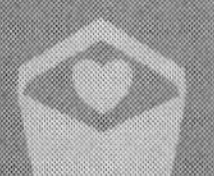

by a new desire–to convert my grueling thesis into a book. For five years, I had been juggling family, work, and school. Was I prepared to tackle the writing scene again? Truthfully, I needed to unwind, so I shelved the book idea. Occasionally, I would sit in front of my computer and attempt to draft a chapter, but my work in Jewish-Christian relations always pulled me away from extensive writing. Yet, in the background, without my knowledge, God was inaugurating *Your Sabbath Invitation.*

The process began after I connected with Emilie and Craig Wierda in 2017, while I was still fully immersed in my ORU thesis. In 2018, God's Divine interruption led Emilie and Craig to sponsor a private gathering between Christian and Jewish leaders to discuss how non-dispensationalist Christians could actualize their support for Israel. In our communications after the gathering, Emilie and Craig often commented that Christian tourism in Israel needed a drastic change. Current template tours are inclined to marginalize the history, culture, and religious practices of the Jewish people. As a result, they inadvertently mask the vital connections between the Land of Israel and the roots of the Christian faith. On the other hand, Emilie and Craig frequently and positively spoke of Ray Vander Laan and the methods he employs to conduct his Israel study tours. Vander Laan is the founder of "That the World May Know Ministries" and creator of the "Faith Lessons" video series. In

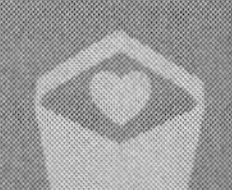

2019, Emilie and Craig invited me to attend their December Israel study tour. I gladly accepted.

On the tour, I learned new ways to experience Israel. In addition, the group's co-leaders, Emilie, Craig, and Pastors Rod and Libby VanSolkema, regularly asked me to contribute a Hebraic perspective to their teachings. Evidently, my contributions impacted the group because Emilie and Craig, for the first time in the history of their tours, decided to observe the Sabbath (*Shabbat*) inside their hotel. Normally, Christian groups reserve Saturday as a day to tour the Dead Sea, Qumran, and Ein Gedi or various sacred Christian sites located in Jerusalem. Instead the group met for prayer and scriptural study. While I was unable to spend *Shabbat* with the group, Emilie's debriefing indicated that something supernatural had occurred.

A few days later, in the back of an Israeli tour bus, Emilie looked at me and said, "We need to write a book on *Shabbat* from a Hebraic perspective." Although I said, "Yes," the monologue in my mind deliberated, "When would I have the time to write a book, especially when I am preparing to host two groups to come to Israel–the United States Christian Academic Mission and the United Methodist Church African Bishops Mission?" Despite my concealed hesitation, Emilie was thrilled that I had said "Yes."

Then, unexpectedly in March 2020, the entire world shut down!

Suddenly, everyone was forced to adjust to a new way of life, both privately and corporately. During the height of the Covid-19 pandemic, a "new normal" emerged, which required additional patience and endurance for every human being to exercise. As a substitute for my customary in-person gatherings, virtual internet meetings became the standard for connecting with friends, family, colleagues, and individuals who have supported the vision concerning Jewish-Christian relations. In spite of the current international tumult, my work and teachings steadily progressed. In fact, after Passover of 2020, as global lockdowns increased, I began to fulfill my commitment to the Wierdas: I started to write a book about *Shabbat*.

After creating initial drafts of the first ten chapters, I received encouraging feedback from my network. At the same time, I sensed that for some individuals in the network, the Hebraic understanding of Scripture was a brand-new revelational journey. Moreover, I realized that I needed an editor to help me "layer" many unfamiliar Jewish topics, concepts, and teaching methods. Therefore, during the 2020 Feast of Tabernacles (September), I contacted Pam Idriss my close friend from my years at ORU. I assumed that

my manuscript was nearly perfect, and I would be able to edit and publish the book within a few weeks. Surprise David! I never expected to relive my thesis experience. Rather than three short weeks of revisions, I was astonished that the book required more chapters, fresh diagrams, a glossary, footnotes, and twelve months of intense work.

In October, I asked Samir Idriss to design the cover and to prepare the entire layout for *Your Sabbath Invitation*. Pamela and Samir were crucial in helping me to dissect and refine multiple concepts in the book. Together we rebuilt the project from its initial vision as a mini-book into the comprehensive form you are reading today.

In March of 2021, after the third country shutdown in Israel, I flew to the United States to meet with Craig, Emilie, Rod, and Libby to discuss the first revision of *Your Sabbath Invitation*. The content that Pamela, Samir, and I conceived genuinely resonated with the group. Just hearing the grunts and sounds of biblical revelation being processed was completely humbling. The late-night phone calls and countless emails, the recurring rabbit holes and profound theological conversations about *Shabbat*, our virtual consultations, and the unhappy in and out editing of insightful nuggets–that eventually failed the final cut–were not in vain! With the assistance and guidance of others, God enabled me to create a completed book.

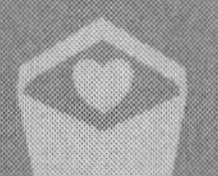

As I recollect the last nineteen months, I have isolated one precious motto:

Never underestimate the power of a conversation on an Israeli bus.

Emilie and Craig, thank you for trusting me and providing your insights and encouragement throughout the process. To Pamela and Samir, I cannot thank you enough. You surpassed my expectations and always demanded excellence in producing this book.

March 2022
Netanya, Israel

PART ONE

What is a Sabbath Invitation

Your Sabbath Invitation

Introduction

Welcome to *Your Sabbath Invitation: Partnership in God's Ultimate Celebration.* As a writer, I am curious what attracted you to my book. Were you searching for an unusual book about the Sabbath? Perhaps the words "*Invitation*" and "*Partnership*" intrigued you, so you thought, "Why and how am I being *invited* to Sabbath, and when did Sabbath become a *partnership*?" If these conditions or something similar applies to you, you have asked the right questions.

To start, there are three main objectives for *Your Sabbath Invitation* : 1) to equip individuals who want to deepen **their relationship with God**, **largely persons with a biblical, Judeo-Christian world view–especially Bible-believing Christians**; 2) to help you **soak in the Amplified Presence of God**, which is accomplished by observing the Sabbath and fulfilling *your partnership* with God; and 3) to empower you to decipher and interpret Scripture in a Hebraic way.

If you are not familiar with the Sabbath, do not worry. Suppose the phrase "Hebraic way" is unfamiliar, stay encouraged. If you are bewildered by "the Amplified Presence of God" and "fulfilling *your partnership* with God," clarity awaits you. *Your Sabbath Invitation* elucidates all of these topics and others such as,

Chapter 5: **"Blessing and Sanctification"**

This chapter offers unique insights for these familiar terms.

Chapter 6: **"God's Original Merciful Act"**

Here, I demonstrate that the Sabbath is more than the seventh day of creation.

Chapter 15: **"Sabbath Anticipation"**

Via Abraham, the Bible explains how we can excitedly look forward to each weekly Sabbath.

Chapter 19: **"Practical Advice for *Shabbat* Beginners"**

The conclusion of the book describes specific practices Christians can implement in their Sabbath celebrations. By the way, as your first, miniature lesson, "*Shabbat*" is the Hebrew word for "Sabbath."

More importantly, the tools you require to process the material are fully included. For instance, without alarming you, *Your Sabbath Invitation* contains a fair amount of Hebrew. Why? The reason is simple–a knowledge of Hebrew is essential for **truly** comprehending the Hebrew Scriptures.

Yet, you are not required to know Hebrew in order to read this book. Halleluyah! I will provide all of the tools you need to navigate the Hebraic **sites** successfully and enjoyably! The only requirement for you is to **get on the bus** and be prepared for an exciting journey.

I emboldened the words **sites** and **bus** because *Your Sabbath Invitation* is both an individual and a group journey. Have you ever been on a tour bus? As a passenger, your primary tasks are to watch, listen, discover, and hopefully to ask questions. As your *literary tour guide*, my chief task is to astonish you with precious "nuggets" from the Bible that concern your relationship with God and the Sabbath. During our trip, I will be a *moreh* (teacher), and you will be *talmidim* (students). Ideally, I do not want you to be passive pupils. Rather, I want you to engage the content vigorously, which is the Jewish method of learning. Even the smallest "nuggets" you collect will be of tremendous value.

Before we begin, let me be honest about the journey. Tour buses offer basic comforts or costly amenities. While the options vary, there is one characteristic every tour possesses: the tourist cannot experience the land or the sites through the window of a bus. **At some point, you will be asked to leave the bus and walk the land**. *Your Sabbath Invitation* is similar. As the guide, I will expect you to leave your comfortable seat and follow me forward. Fortunately, the *Nekrutman Sabbath Tour Services* will equip you to engage the terrain and explore the sites before you.

Here are some provisions that will facilitate the trip:

- The phrase "Author's translation" occurs throughout *Your Sabbath Invitation* and indicates that the author translated the verse. The term represents the author's scholastic ability and earned permission to translate biblical passages. The Glossary provides a comprehensive definition.
- Numbered footnotes at the bottom of the page offer significant details. Please read them!
- To keep the journey exciting, most chapters in the book are short and contain multiple tables, illustrations, and callouts.
- Chapter highlights begin each chapter and note pages conclude each chapter.
- A Glossary provides more information for especially unfamiliar words and terms.
- To help you recognize, read, and pronounce a foreign word, *Your Sabbath Invitation* supplies a combined transliteration and transcription–in parentheses–beside every Hebrew, Aramaic, and Greek word. Consult the Glossary for an explanation of transliteration and transcription.
- A list of selected Hebrew Words with their pronunciations and definitions will be found at the back of the book.

- An Appendix expands important material that is too weighty to discuss in the main text.

It is almost time for departure. I have two final comments. I composed *Your Sabbath Invitation* **to invite, educate, and motivate you to experience *the Amplified Presence of God on the Sabbath.* From the beginning, God has always intended for humanity to observe and participate in the Sabbath.** I am inviting you to join me on a journey of discovery.

Lastly, the Bible verse which inspired my book is Isaiah 66:23. The verse prophesies that at the end of time, all people who are serving God throughout the world–Jewish and non-Jewish–will be participating in the Sabbath. *Your Sabbath Invitation* is intended to assist you in the fulfillment of this special "appointed time."

Now, please gather your briefcases, backpacks, and your favorite Bible version and board the bus. The first stop is an exploration of Isaiah 66:23 and the Messianic Age.

Chapter 1 Highlights

- A peaceful scenario exists for the end of time.
- Isaiah 66:23 prophesied that during the Messianic Age all nations will observe the Sabbath.
- The Sabbath is as old as humanity. It is meant for all who believe in the God of Abraham, Issac, and Jacob. Conversion to Judaism is not required for observance.
- Sabbath is integral to a godly lifestyle. It is not instantaneous; it is an on-going process.
- The Sabbath state of mind is God-centered and free from worry about personal needs.
- A segment of Christendom is already valuing the Judaism of Jesus and choosing to share their destiny with the Jewish people.

Your Sabbath Invitation

The Messianic Sabbath

***"'And it will be that from New Moon to New Moon, from Shabbat to Shabbat, all of humanity will worship before Me,' says The Eternal."*[1]**

Isaiah 66:23 (Author's translation)

I assume that many of you are familiar with popular end of time scenarios that include prophecies about wars, famines, plagues, natural disasters, false prophets, and the outpouring of God's Spirit. The scenarios will vary depending on an individual's eschatological and theological views and on their interpretation of the Book

[1]Unless otherwise indicated, all Scripture quotations in *Your Sabbath Invitation* are from The Holy Bible, New International Version® NIV® Copyright © 1973, 1978, 1984, 2011 by Biblica, Inc.™ Used by permission. All rights reserved worldwide.

of Revelation. Based on the globalization of the world and the turbulent times in which we are living, I should not be surprised when Bible teachers and passionate writers focus on these cataclysmic incidents. At the same time, I am also aware that not all Christians subscribe to an end of time packed with disastrous events.

Within the context of most of these teachings I have never even heard Sabbath observance mentioned. Christian radio and television, social media and printed platforms–all are predominantly silent. Frankly, I am not surprised or discouraged because Jews and Christians view and handle the Sabbath quite differently.[2] In *Your Sabbath Invitation*, I will show you that behind all the conversations and apart from all the commotion, a peaceful scenario exists. I will explore Isaiah 66:23 and demonstrate that Sabbath observance is directly related to the end of time, and the coming of the messiah (Messiah).[3]

But let us first step back to Isaiah 1, where God clearly reprimands the children of Israel for their religious hypocrisy, and specifically, for not observing the Sabbath. When we reach Isaiah 66:1–5, the nation is again rebuked for living a socially immoral life, for maintaining an ungodly marketplace, and for violating religious rituals. In stark contrast, the last half of chapter 66 records prophesies of a reborn Jerusalem, with every nation rejoicing in the city's restoration and in their own national privilege of seeing

---

[2]Certain Christians, such as Seventh-Day Adventists, do regard Friday evening to Saturday evening as the Sabbath.

[3]In *Your Sabbath Invitation*, the "Messianic Age" and the "end of time" represent the same period. Please see the Glossary.

God's glory. Isaiah 66:23 concludes the chapter with Israel and all the nations worshiping God on the New Moon and on the Sabbath, even as the rebellious receive their punishment.[4] Surely, Sabbath is the peaceful scenario for the end of time!

Let me now repeat, as an Orthodox Jew involved in the sacred calling to advance Jewish-Christian relations, I do not expect you to convert to Judaism or practice Judaism's customary approaches to the Sabbath.[5] **Instead, I desire for you to view Sabbath as an attractive integral part of a godly lifestyle.** Jews and Christians both know that Sabbath is as old as humanity. After all, during the creation week, humanity's arrival and the Sabbath are only one day apart![6] Additionally, Sabbath Day observance predated the

---

[4]Within the context of Isaiah 66, the phrase "all mankind" (all of humanity, Author's translation) **only** includes people who *obey* The Eternal. Verse 66:2 mentions the "humble," the "contrite in spirit," and persons who "tremble" at His word.

[5]After the destruction of the Second Temple in 70 CE and the failure of the *Bar Kokhba* revolt in 132–136 CE, Jews lost complete jurisdictional sovereignty over the land of Israel. Most Jews began to be dispersed around the world and a remnant remained in the northern part of Israel. Rebuilding Judaism would be improbable without the key elements of any successful civilization such as, large population centers, monumental architecture, and governing systems for administering territories. However, through God's word, the Torah, Judaism was able to rebuild and sustain itself through almost 2,000 years of exile. During this mammoth transformation of restoring, reestablishing, and relocating the Jewish people, *Shabbat* observance was inexorably affixed to our indomitable history. Without a doubt, the Sabbath saved Judaism!

[6]Humanity was created on the sixth day, and the Sabbath was created *as* the seventh day arrived (see chapter 13). According to Psalm 90:4, humanity and the Sabbath could be separated by as much as 1000 years. Regardless, they are ancient!

giving of the Torah at Sinai.[7] In the Book of Genesis, the Sabbath was the first element in creation that God called *holy*. In the Messianic Age, all of humanity will observe the sacred day.[8]

Your Sabbath journey has decidedly launched, so let me challenge you with a "maiden voyage" question: "When and how will Isaiah's Sabbath prophecy be observed by the nations?" Some of you might respond, "David, because of the *suddenness* implied by Isaiah 66:23, the prophecy could only be fulfilled during the *culmination* of the Messianic Age. Reading 'from one Sabbath to another, all mankind will come and bow down before me,' I see an immediate universal event."

Understandably, deferring the prophecy's outcome to a distant future is logical because its *sudden* fulfillment today is almost unimaginable. Nonetheless, **I propose that Isaiah 66:23 is not reserved for the future. I submit that the prophecy is being fulfilled *now*–as individuals around the world *learn to observe* the Sabbath one at a time. Sabbath is an individual and global *process*.**

A meaningful Sabbath is brewed and voluntary. ***It is NOT instant coffee!***

The Sabbath celebration is not instant coffee, neither is it a member of our autonomic nervous system.[9] A

---

[7]See "Torah" in the Glossary.

[8]Most Orthodox Jewish Zionists believe the Messianic Age is now. In *Your Sabbath Invitation*, the "Messianic Age" and the "end of time" represent the same period. Please see "end of time" in the Glossary.

[9]See "autonomic nervous system" in the Glossary.

meaningful Sabbath is brewed and voluntary. Time and deliberate actions are prerequisites for understanding the Sabbath *and* for implementing Sabbath celebrations with awe. Perhaps now is an ideal time to start integrating Sabbath into your life!

I identified Sabbath as a "process" because processes are featured throughout the Scriptures. For example, at the beginning of Genesis, the Bible plainly establishes monogamy as the ideal design for marriage: "That is why a man leaves his father and mother and is united to his wife, and they become one flesh" (Genesis 2:24). Yet, God's mandate required thousands of years–a *process*–to obtain global acceptance amidst societies and cultures that were rooted in polygamy.

Like marriage, the Sabbath has faced a comparable setback. God originated the Sabbath, but humanity obeyed, ignored, and dishonored the Sabbath. Currently, only a fraction of humanity celebrates the Sabbath. Eventually, according to Isaiah 66:23, *all* of humanity will obey the Sabbath and satisfy God's original intentions. If observing the Sabbath is a process, then restoring the Sabbath is also a process. Both require time, education, and participation to accomplish Isaiah's prophecy.

It is possible that ignorance and misunderstanding have spawned negative views of the Sabbath. As a Christian, you may be hesitant to accept an invitation to fulfill Isaiah's Sabbath celebration. Here are some potential reasons:

- The Sabbath may disrupt your present routine and schedule.

- The uncertainty of what Sabbath observance entails lessens its appeal and prevents you from becoming a participant.
- As a believer in Jesus, you may feel unable to partner in the fulfillment of the Sabbath prophecy.
- Sabbath has always been presented as a strictly Jewish observance, which renders it too law-oriented for you to consider.

There is a Jewish maxim that says, "You are not required to complete the work, but you are not at liberty to stand idly by."[10] To rephrase, you can actively participate in God's redemptive process and purposes because you are not here to finish the entire Sabbath task. As a minimum, you can initiate the assignment.

Your Sabbath Invitation is composed from a Hebraic perspective, and we will be decoding Hebrew biblical texts to discover a variety of Sabbath messages. I do believe that Sabbath observance should begin Friday evening and conclude Saturday evening (Jewish biblical days begin in the evening). In no way am I advocating a removal of Sunday worship services.[11] The Sabbath is not contingent upon Church services. In addition, allow me to clarify that

---

[10]m. Avot 2.16, *Sage Advice Pirkei Avot*, trans. Irving Greenberg (Jerusalem: Maggid Books, 2016), 103.

[11]I have found that most Christians view Sunday as the weekend, a day of rest, or as the Sabbath. Instead, for Orthodox Jews living in Israel, Saturday represents both the Sabbath and the weekend because Sunday is the first day of the work week in Israel.

the Sabbath journey you are considering or investigating does not entail a path to financial success, improved personal health, or the healing of emotional pains. Certainly, it is possible that while observing the Sabbath, you may experience some or all of these blessings. Notwithstanding, the Sabbath is independent of our emotions, physical condition, desires, and current needs. **The Sabbath is HIS TIME! The Sabbath is God-centered. *Your Sabbath Invitation* will focus on how we prepare ourselves to enter into a Sabbath state of mind–to be enveloped in a sanctified period, free of worry and anxiety about our needs.** The Sabbath is a unique day to seek Him! This day is like no other!

As I guide you into a Hebraic perspective of the Sabbath and its correlation to the end of time–via texts within the Books of Genesis, Exodus, Psalms and Isaiah–I must also mention Israel, yesterday and today. How does modern-day Israel fit into Sabbath prophecy? In Isaiah 66, which describes people across the world celebrating the Sabbath, Isaiah also prophesies the sovereignty of the Jewish people over the Land of Israel, "...Can a country be born in a day or a nation be brought forth in a moment?" (Isaiah 66:8). On Friday, May 14, 1948 (the 5th day of the Hebrew month of *Iyar* in the Jewish calendar year of 5708), when David Ben-Gurion declared Israel's statehood, Isaiah 66:8 began its fulfillment.

In one moment, Jewish sovereignty was reborn in the Land of Israel, but the rebirth was not incidental. Israel's restoration involved almost 1,900 years of exilic prayers, unanticipated Divine agents within the various Zionist movements prior to statehood, and a geopolitical moment when many nations ultimately accepted a Jewish state. The miracle also required bloodshed and sacrifices of tens of thousands to ensure that the vitality of the State of Israel would continue after 1948. The task has never been effortless or trouble-free. Since 1948, Israel has been surrounded by enemies on her borders and has been repeatedly marginalized on the world stage. Despite countless adversities, God continues to ensure that His will shall be done in the modern chapters of sacred history.

*A segment is valuing the **Judaism of Jesus**!*

We are living in unparalleled times, when once envisioned prophecies are being actualized today. I do not believe the emergence of the State of Israel and the advent of a new era in which more Christians are exploring the Jewish roots of their faith are coincidental events. **Today, a segment of Christendom is valuing the Judaism of Jesus, and is steadily growing in numbers and in knowledge as each Christian endeavors to walk with the God of Abraham, Isaac, and Jacob. This fervent body of believers does not intend to co-opt biblical practices from the Jewish people, but rather to enhance and share their own destiny with the people who are considered to be the "apple of God's eye."**[12]

Currently, you may or may not be associated with this particular segment, but for some reason you have chosen to

[12]Zechariah 2:8.

read *Your Sabbath Invitation.* Even this is not a coincidence. You are part of the new miracle, where God is pouring out His Spirit so that you might know Him in a more profound way.

Notes

Chapter 2 Highlights

- The Heavenly Torah existed prior to the Torah at Sinai (Exodus 20).
- Torah is a "code" that needs to be deciphered. Revelations must be "mined" from the biblical text.
- Knowledge of Biblical Hebrew and Hebraic interpretation are essential for mining revelations.
- The preferred definition of "Torah" is "instructions."
- The Heavenly Torah is the perfect, invisible form of the earthly Torah.
- The alternative Hebrew word for "I" (*Ano'chi*) teaches us that metaphorically, the Torah is God's soul. The earthly Torah connects to the Heavenly Torah.
- We experience a God-soul moment when we receive revelation from the text.
- From the very beginning, God intended for all humanity to celebrate the Sabbath.

Your Sabbath Invitation

Mining Torah Revelation

e are privileged to live in an era when Bibles are available in multiple forms. We can purchase Bibles in assorted book formats from local stores and supermarkets. We can access hundreds of versions and translations on our phones–visibly and audibly! Remarkably, we have online access to numerous Bible and Jewish commentaries that have been composed throughout the centuries. Universities and colleges worldwide have biblical studies departments, and it is easier than ever to fly across continents to view and experience the geography of the Bible. In spite of the unlimited, high technology, *push-button* access to the Scriptures in our day, everyone does not understand the origin and transmission history of the Bible. In fact, some may assume that the Bible has always existed and **only** existed in some physical format, beginning with Moses and the stone tablets. At this moment, you recognize my routine: "David intends to dislodge our misconceptions once again. No problem David! We are ready, eager, and open!" My response is "Excellent!"

Although the giving of the Torah at Sinai occurred 3,500 years ago, the Heavenly Torah already existed prior to Exodus 20. Committed Jews believe that God created the Torah and used it to fashion the world. For Christians reading *Your Sabbath Invitation* this statement should not shock you because the first words in the Gospel of John are: "In the beginning was the Word" (John 1:1a, Author's translation). At the time the Gospel was written, Jews already understood that the Torah pre-existed prior to its physical manifestation on the earth.

*Torah existed **before** the world was created!*

Regarding the Hebrew Bible, Orthodox Jews revere every word and vowel point as sacred. Reading the Torah is equivalent to hearing God's exact words. We also believe Torah revelation is infinite because the Torah originates from an infinite being–God. However, **God's infinite revelation is coded within the finite words of the Bible. To decipher the code, we must "mine revelations" from the words in the biblical text, as if we were mining gold.** In a spiritual sense, the phrase is accurate and telling because the word of God has inestimable value.

*Torah is a **code** that needs to be **deciphered**.*

Mining revelation from the Hebrew Bible requires a knowledge of Biblical Hebrew and an understanding of the Hebraic principles of scriptural interpretation. We will be mining revelation throughout *Your Sabbath Invitation* to enhance our comprehension of Scriptures that explicitly or implicitly apply to the Sabbath. Mining revelation is not easy, but it is always fascinating! In this chapter, I will teach you how to mine using a rich passage from the Hebrew Bible (Torah)–Exodus 20:2.

Torah is much more than law. It is best defined as "instructions"!

Without delay, to avoid confusion, let me define the words "Torah" and "Heavenly Torah." Clarity is essential because Torah and Heavenly Torah are vital, recurring topics in *Your Sabbath Invitation*. **For many outside of Judaism, Torah probably signifies "law," "laws," or "The Law," although the preferred and correct Jewish understanding is "instructions." The *Torah* represents** 1) the first five Books of Moses; 2) a general term for all of God's instructions, requirements, laws, and commandments; 3) the entire written and canonized Hebrew Bible; or 4) specific passages or verses. **The *Heavenly Torah* refers to the invisible, unwritten form of our *earthly* Torah.** Heavenly Torah is eternal, perfect, and unchanging. It existed before its physical delivery at Mount Sinai. Ultimately, context will determine the pertinent definition for the Hebrew term "Torah."

Table 1 contains Exodus 20:2 (see next page), which introduces the Ten Commandments (or as I prefer, the Ten Categorical Statements).

Talmidim (students), Table 1 is your first encounter with Hebrew. Write this down! **Hebrew and Aramaic are read from right to left, not left to right.** Now, find the Hebrew word **אָנֹכִי** (*Ano'chi*), which means "I" in English.

Table 1. Exodus 20:2

"**I** am the LORD your God, who brought you out of Egypt, out of the land of slavery." (Exodus 20:2)	***Ano'chi*** *Ado'nai*[1] *E'lo'heh'cha asher ho'tze'ticha me'eretz Mitz'ra'yim me'bet avadim.*	**אָנֹכִי** יְהוָה אֱלֹהֶיךָ אֲשֶׁר הוֹצֵאתִיךָ מֵאֶרֶץ מִצְרַיִם מִבֵּית עֲבָדִים.

Repeatedly, the Hebrew Scriptures use two terms for "I"—"**אֲנִי**" (*Ani*) and "**אָנֹכִי**" (*Ano'chi*). "*Ani*" is the preferred, mainstream word for "I" throughout the Bible. This fact generates a crucial question: **Why did God use the alternative term *Ano'chi* in the opening of the Ten Commandments (Ten Categorical Statements) instead of the mainstream expression *Ani*?**

The answer is both simple and profound. The Hebrew **אָנֹכִי** (*Ano'chi*) is more than just a translation of the word "I"; it is also an acronym which forms the Aramaic expression "**אנא נפשי כתבית יהבית**" (*Ana Naf'shi K'ta'vit Y'ha'vit*). The beginning letters of each word of the phrase match the letters that spell **אָנֹכִי** (*Ano'chi*). Table 2 shows the relationship.

---

[1]The Hebrew term "*Adonai*" is a substitution for "יְהוָה" that Orthodox Jews pronounce whenever they are reading from the Torah Scroll or praying. When Jews are learning or teaching from the Hebrew Bible, they use the term "*HaShem*" ("The Name") as a replacement for "יְהוָה." See Appendix A-3, "The Transcription *Adonai* as a Substitute for The Tetragrammaton."

Table 2. The אָנֹכִי (*Ano'chi*) Acronym (read right to left)

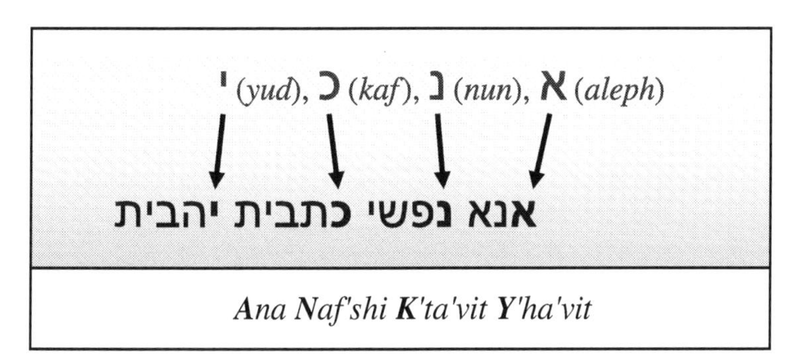

*Ana Naf'shi **K**'ta'vit **Y**'ha'vit*

This expression appears in an ancient rabbinic commentary.[2] I translated "אנא נפשי כתבית יהבית" for you here:

"I wrote down My very Soul and gave it to you."

The *Ano'chi* acronym provides significant relational insight between God and Torah. More than just a record of considerable episodes from humanity's beginnings, Israel's history, and God's commandments, **the Torah, metaphorically speaking, is God's soul. Our canonized, finite, written Torah connects to the Heavenly Torah.**

---

[2]The expression is found in the Babylonian Talmud (b. Shabbat 105a). The Babylonian Talmud is written in Aramaic, however, the Aramaic language uses Hebrew letters! Hebrew and Aramaic are both Semitic languages; they share numerous commonalities in the areas of grammar, linguistics, morphology, and etymology. Further discussion exceeds the limits of *Your Sabbath Invitation*. Nonetheless, the אָנֹכִי (*Ano'chi*) acronym is still viable for mining revelation because the Babylonian Talmud is an authoritative Jewish source. See "Babylonian Talmud" in the Glossary.

When we engage in His word, we are wrapped in the soul of God! **If we learn a new revelation from the Torah, *and a light bulb suddenly turns on within us*, then we experience a God-soul moment.** God speaks to us when we engage in His word.

A God-soul moment** is the revelation received **when we engage the text.

By using the alternative expression of the word "I" (*Ano'chi*) in Exodus 20:2, God hinted to us that the Ten Commandments (Ten Categorical Statements) are more than just words on a stone tablet. **The Jewish nation was going to receive the real operating system of the world, the Torah, and simultaneously connect to God in a more profound way than ever before**.

Up to this point, you have learned that decoding the Hebrew enables an individual to connect with the Heavenly Torah and to attain revelation from Scripture. The revelation is equivalent to a God-soul moment. Nevertheless, you may still ask, "What does this have to do with the Sabbath?" Many still think that the Sabbath was originally mandated at Sinai with the Ten Commandments (Ten Categorical Statements). This is definitely incorrect! **As we continue to decode the finite texts of the Hebrew Bible *prior* to Exodus 20, we will discover that from the very beginning, God intended for *all humanity* to celebrate the Sabbath!**

Notes

Chapter 3 Highlights

- Time is important for humanity. Genesis 1-11 records the first 2,000 years of human history including, births, deaths, ages, and lineages.
- The Hebrew word "*mo'a'dim*" means "appointed times."
- Appointed times are Divine engagements.
- In Genesis 1:14, God spoke lights into the sky as signs for *mo'a'dim*.
- *Z'man* and *et* are two other Hebrew words for time.
- *Mo'a'dim* are not random. God uses *mo'a'dim* for the biblical holidays (Leviticus 23). The Sabbath is the mother of all *mo'a'dim*.
- Each week God has scheduled an appointment with you, as a rhythm of life that demonstrates His unchanging character.
- The Sabbath is not about "do's" and "do not's." It is about our willingness to develop a Sabbath state of mind.

Your Sabbath Invitation

A Study in Time

ave you ever considered how we use the word "time" in our daily language? For many, time works like a pressure cooker. At work we say, "It is crunch time" and "The clock is ticking." We regularly hope that "deadlines" will be met. As a former New Yorker, I remember the expression from my bosses that demanded a project to be done in a "New York minute." In our microwave era, we are always looking for gadgets that will "save time" so we can "make time" for family and friends. As "time goes by," we are amazed at how "time flies." Nevertheless, no matter what we do, we still seem to fall behind.

As teenagers, we frequently viewed our parents as old-fashioned and "behind the times." Perhaps, we admired people who were jetsetters and "ahead of their time." For the transition into our adult years, we started praying to "hit the big time" so we could enjoy all of life's pleasures. As some approach potential mid-life crises, they might regret never "spending time" with the ones they love. And the last expression anyone wants to hear from a doctor is "your days are numbered."

It seems impossible, but "there was a time" when the world was not "24/7." With the advent of the internet and our online shopping culture, we now enjoy "one click ordering." Our world is "working around the clock." Above all, two of the worst sayings in contemporary language are the claims to "waste time" or to "kill time." Figuratively, I equate both of these expressions with first-degree murder! Even Moses wrote, "Teach us to number our days, that we may gain a heart of wisdom" (Psalm 90:12).

Let us never forget that the first 2,000 years of human history are summarized in Genesis 1–11. Chapters 5 and 10 highlight the births, deaths, and ages of people, and chapter 11 accentuates Shem's lineage. Evidently, time was meaningful to humanity before God elected Abraham in Genesis 12. In fact, prior to the Exodus from Egypt, it is probable that human beings already had appointed times to commune with God the Creator.

Appointed Times Biblically Defined as Mo'a'dim

> ***"Mo'a'dim" are appointed times.***

Time is the theme for chapter 3 and Sabbath is the theme of *Your Sabbath Invitation*. When we study time and the Sabbath together, we must include the "appointed times." **The Hebrew word for appointed times is מוֹעֲדִים** (*mo'a'dim*). Appointed times are Divine engagements.

Although God classified the Sabbath as one of His appointed times in Leviticus 23:2, He previously embedded the concept of "appointed times" in Genesis 1:14. Read Table 3 below:

Table 3. Genesis 1:14

"And God said, 'Let there be lights in the vault of the sky to separate the day from the night, and let them serve as signs to mark **sacred times**, and days and years…'"	*Va'yo'mare Elohim, y'he m'o'rot bir'key'a ha'sha'mayim, l'hav'dil bein hayom oo'bein ha'lye'la, v'ha'yu l'o'toat* ***oo'l'mo'a'dim*** *oo'l'ya'mim v'sha'nim*	וַיֹּאמֶר אֱלֹהִים יְהִי מְאֹרֹת בִּרְקִיעַ הַשָּׁמַיִם לְהַבְדִּיל בֵּין הַיּוֹם וּבֵין הַלָּיְלָה וְהָיוּ לְאֹתֹת **וּלְמוֹעֲדִים** וּלְיָמִים וְשָׁנִים

In Table 3, the NIV® 2011 translates the Hebrew term **מוֹעֲדִים** (*mo'a'dim*) as "sacred times." Most English Bible translations define *mo'a'dim* as "seasons." I purposely translated *mo'a'dim* as "appointed times" because there are other Hebrew words that signify time, namely **זְמָנִים** (*z'ma'nim*) and **עִתִּים** (*e'tim*).

As I stated earlier, Orthodox Jews revere every word in the Torah; each term has significance. God deliberately chose *mo'a'dim* in Genesis 1:14, and we must determine why. So, we will conduct a scriptural exploration of all three Hebrew terms–*z'ma'nim*, *e'tim*, and *mo'a'dim.*

1 זְמָנִים (*z'ma'nim*)

The singular form of **זְמָנִים** (*z'ma'nim*) is "**זְמָן**" (*z'man*). The Hebrew Bible contains variations of **זְמָן** written in Hebrew and Aramaic. The **exact word** *z'man* only appears twice in the Hebrew language (Nehemiah 2:6, Ecclesiastes 3:1). Together, Esther 9:27 and 9:31 contain two different forms of **זְמָן**. The remaining variations of *z'man* are in Aramaic alone. The word *z'man* refers to a specific span of time as in Nehemiah 2:6, "Then the king, with the queen sitting beside him, asked me, 'How long will your journey take, and when will you get back?' It pleased the king to send me; so I set a **time** (*z'man*)."

2 עִתִּים (*e'tim*)

The singular form of **עִתִּים** (*e'tim*) is "**עֵת**" (*et*). The word *et* has two special meanings:

- *Point in time* as in Genesis 24:11, "And he caused the camels to kneel from outside the town by a well of water at the **time** (**לְעֵת**, *l'et*) of evening at the **time** (**לְעֵת**, *l'et*) the women who are drawing water go forth (Author's translation).
- *Duration of time* as in Deuteronomy 1:18, "And at that **time** (***et***) I told you everything you were to do."

3 מוֹעֲדִים (*mo'a'dim*)

The last term is מוֹעֲדִים (*mo'a'dim*); its singular form is "מוֹעֵד" (*mo'ed*, time). Within the context of time, a *mo'ed* is something that is scheduled by God or by a human being. Please note that in Genesis, God tells Abraham exactly when Isaac will be born, and He expresses it as a "מוֹעֵד" (*mo'ed*, time): "But my covenant I will establish with Isaac, whom Sarah will bear to you by this **time** (*mo'ed*) next year" (Genesis 17:21).

Why have I dedicated so much *time* identifying and distinguishing the Hebrew words that are translated as "time" and "times" in English? I distinguish because the Scriptures do! The *mo'a'dim* are not random times. When God introduces the biblical holidays of Passover, the Feast of Tabernacles, and others in Leviticus 23, He designates them as *mo'a'dim.* This also includes the Sabbath:

> "Speak to the children of Israel, and say to them: 'The Eternal appointed that you should declare as holy occasions. These are My appointed [times]. Six days work (*me'la'cha*) can be done; on the seventh day is a *Shabbat Shabbaton*, a holy occasion where no work (*me'la'cha*) can be done. It is a *Shabbat* to The Eternal in all your residences'" (Leviticus 23:2–3, Author's translation).

When God sets the Sabbath apart from the other holidays, Sabbath becomes the mother of all *mo'a'dim*.

> *Sabbath is the mother of all mo'a'dim (appointed times).*

From the time of creation, God has been scheduling humanity to be with Him on the Sabbath. **This means, each week, God has an appointment with you**, not as a work-related task, but *as a rhythm of life* that demonstrates the unchanging character of God.

> *The Sabbath appointment **is a rhythm of life.***

As you consider the Sabbath invitation, may I propose a humble suggestion for you: In the Friday evening to Saturday evening date boxes of your calendar write, **"This is my Sabbath time with God."**[1]

> ***Just as God keeps us in His calendar, we can keep Him in ours.***

Previously, I stated that the Sabbath was about Him and our willingness **to be in His appointed Presence**. **The theology of the Sabbath** is not predicated on a list of "do's" and "do not's," but rather on ***developing a Sabbath state of mind***.

---

[1]On October 5, 2020, I enjoyed a lengthy conversation with Rabbi Reuven Chaim Klein. The October discussion and my previous visit to his August 30, 2020 blog contributed to my inspiration regarding *z'man*, *et*, and *mo'ed*. See Chaim Klein, "Trends in Time," The Blogs (blog), The Times of Israel, August 30, 2020, https://blogs. timesofisrael.com/ trends-in-time/ (4 October 2021).

Notes

Chapter 4 Highlights

- The word "Sabbath" is the English derivation of the Hebrew word "*Shabbat*."
- The meaning of *Shabbat* exceeds simple English definitions. *Shabbat* is *Shabbat*.
- "Exegesis" discovers the meaning of words. Exegesis is a subset of "hermeneutics," the art and science of biblical interpretation.
- Hermeneutics are essential for understanding the Bible, but Christian and Jewish hermeneutics differ.
- From ancient to modern times, the number of days in a week has varied.
- A seven-day week comes from God and is non-negotiable. *Shabbat* confines a week to seven days.
- God finished making order out of chaos during the initial six days of creation.
- *Shabbat*, the seventh day, is distinct. God "blessed" and "sanctified" *Shabbat*.

Your Sabbath Invitation

The Week Link

So far in *Your Sabbath Invitation*, I have primarily used the word Sabbath. As we continue our journey together, I will be using the term *Shabbat* (שַׁבָּת). The word Sabbath is the English derivation of *Shabbat*; Sabbath has linguistic origins in Hebrew, Greek, Latin, and Old English. Sabbath and *Shabbat* are used interchangeably throughout *Your Sabbath Invitation*, **so please become accustomed to both terms.** While the terms share the same definitions, ***Shabbat* (שַׁבָּת) is more meaningful** and is generally preferred whenever we are decoding, excavating, and interpreting certain Hebrew terms.

Hebrew is read from right to left. The term Shabbat with vowels looks like this: שַׁבָּת. It consists of three Hebrew letters: Shin (ש), Bet (ב), and Taf (ת).

Many dictionaries define Sabbath as a specific day for a faith community to rest, to worship, or to do both, but scripturally speaking, the term *Shabbat* cannot be translated with a solitary English word, such as "rest." To the contrary, ***Shabbat* is packed with biblical nuances that exceed simple definitions**. For Jews, *Shabbat* is *Shabbat*!

> *Shabbat cannot be translated with a solitary English word.*
> ***Shabbat is Shabbat !***

I hope you are enjoying your Sabbath journey because you are about to encounter your **first academic *detour***. Above, I mentioned a trio of technical terms, "decoding, excavating, and interpreting." The term "decoding" specifically applies to Hebrew words. We do not decode English words! Likewise, we do not excavate English words! The word "excavating" and other forms such as, "excavate" and "excavation," occur over fifty times in *Your Sabbath Invitation*. To excavate is to dig for a specific objective. Archaeologists *excavate* to *unearth* ancient artifacts, ruins, or buildings. **In *Your Sabbath Invitation*, we *excavate* to *uncover* ancient revelations buried in the Hebrew Bible and to obtain new revelations and insights. For us, "excavating" is the process of mining revelation from the Torah.**

Surely, all of you understand the third term "interpreting," which usually means "to explain" or "to translate." Biblical interpretation is more complex and consists of two fundamental terms–"exegesis" and "hermeneutics." *Exegesis* is the act and process of discovering the meaning of a word in its original context, environment, and setting.[1] The focus in *Your Sabbath Invitation* is biblical exegesis, so our goal is to determine how the Bible's original speakers and listeners heard and understood specific words and phrases. As you might expect, a thorough exegesis of the Hebrew Scriptures requires a knowledge of Biblical Hebrew, but be encouraged. The exegesis in this book has been specifically adapted for you. I always include the English transliteration, translation, or the most accurate English equivalent of every Hebrew word.[2] This is one reason why I asked you to become comfortable with the Hebrew word *Shabbat*!

Hermeneutics is related to exegesis; the terms are almost inseparable, and the common goal for both is "interpretation." Hermeneutics is the broad science and art of interpretation.[3] It includes exegesis, specific rules, and established scholarly techniques that one applies in order to interpret a text.[4] *Notice that exegesis is a subset of hermeneutics.* Biblical

---

[1]See the Glossary for an extended definition of "exegesis."

[2]Transliteration is a method that adapts a foreign word from its *own* language into *another* language using the alphabet of the *other* language. Transliterations enable people to read or pronounce foreign words in their *own native* language or *another* language. In *Your Sabbath Invitation*, Hebrew words written with Hebrew letters are *transliterated* into English using the English alphabet. See the Glossary entry "transcription, translation, transliteration" for more information.

[3]The word "art" refers to how insightfully a person applies the techniques and rules of hermeneutics.

[4]Here, I have only provided cursory definitions. Technically, the terms exegesis and hermeneutics pertain to any literary work although they are principally associated with biblical studies. Exegesis and hermeneutics are essential for concentrated Bible study. A quality

hermeneutics is an essential discipline and is usually a required course in accredited Christian seminaries.[5] In *Your Sabbath Invitation*, I will be introducing you to Jewish hermeneutics **because Christian and Jewish hermeneutics differ**. Wait! All is well! Jewish exegesis promises a satisfying journey and an opportunity to uncover great revelations.

Informed readers, the academic detour just ended. Let us return to our journey and investigate how to comprehend the Hebrew word *Shabbat*. Remember, the Hebrew word *Shabbat* corresponds to the English word Sabbath.

Most of you are already aware that Sabbath occurs at the end of the week. Others may assign Sabbath to a another day, such as Monday or Wednesday. For a moment, consider the number of days in a week. Do you automatically conclude that seven days have always been the universal standard for a week? You may be surprised that in many ancient civilizations weeks were not necessarily composed of seven days.

---

exegesis requires time and a variety of literary tools such as, dictionaries, lexicons (language dictionaries), commentaries, encyclopedias, and more. Hermeneutics preclude haphazard and overly subjective interpretations of a biblical text. For centuries, Jews and Christians have been utilizing hermeneutics that are accepted and grounded within each respective tradition. **Hence, Jewish and Christian hermeneutics are not entirely identical.** Nonetheless, both Jews and Christians seek to maintain firm standards and rules that guard the Bible from spurious interpretations. Consider a deeper study of biblical hermeneutics.

[5]I know directly because I exegeted many Bible verses when I attended seminary! Read an overview of my thesis experience during seminary in the Preface of *Your Sabbath Invitation*.

The Egyptian calendar included ten days in a week. The Assyrians established five days, and Ancient Rome chose eight. Even the Aztecs developed a hefty thirteen-day week. What about contemporary civilizations? Has any nation or country within the last three hundred years attempted to alter our seven-day week? The answer may alarm you.

The Egyptians, Assyrians, Romans, and Aztecs never had a Sabbath!

To eradicate religious and monarchial influences from French society during the later years of the French Revolution, France adopted a Republican Calendar.[6] This calendar had ten days in a week. The idea only lasted for a dozen years until Napoleon abolished it.

Joseph Stalin of Russia pursued another direction by imposing a six-day week to wean out any religious influences in his country. So, when you read about the creation of the world in the Bible, you should be shocked by the number of days in a week! **Apparently, a seven-day week has been treated as a negotiable unit in multiple human societies,**

The seven-day week comes from God!

[6]The term "Republican" refers to its application in France during the late eighteenth and early nineteenth centuries. French citizens sought a new form of government which would prioritize the issues of "public" citizens and remove medieval (feudal) land and economic policies that favored the monarchy. Therefore, the designation "Republican Calendar" is not associated with an American Republican calendar, which has never existed!

but a biblical *Shabbat* intrinsically confines a week to seven days.

The idea that *Shabbat* restricts a week to seven days is profoundly important. Genesis 1–2 describes God's creative events according to individual days. After a creative event occurs, the number of the day is indicated. Each day of creation exhibited more order than the previous day.

Genesis 1:2 affirms that the world began in a state of chaos, and Genesis 2:2 confirms that everything is in order prior to the seventh day. In Table 4, Genesis 2:2 can be reviewed in Hebrew, in the English transliteration, and in its English translation.

Table 4. Genesis 2:2 (Author's translation)

And *Elohim* completed with the seventh day His work that He did, and He ceased (וַיִּשְׁבֹּת, *va'yish'boat*) with the seventh day from all His work that He did.	*Va'yi'chal Elohim ba'yom ha'sh'vi'e m'lach'to asher asah,* ***va'yish'boat*** *ba'yom ha'sh'vi'e me'kol m'lach'toe asher asah*	וַיְכַל אֱלֹהִים בַּיּוֹם הַשְּׁבִיעִי מְלַאכְתּוֹ אֲשֶׁר עָשָׂה **וַיִּשְׁבֹּת** בַּיּוֹם הַשְּׁבִיעִי מִכָּל־מְלַאכְתּוֹ אֲשֶׁר עָשָׂה

In Table 4, observe that one Hebrew word, **וַיִּשְׁבֹּת**, is in bold. This word is pronounced *va'yish'boat*. The word **וַיִּשְׁבֹּת** (*va'yish'boat*) contains the same letters as **שַׁבָּת** (*Shabbat*)! Although the seventh day is not coined *Shabbat* until Exodus 16:23, you can observe via the Hebrew in

Genesis 2:2 that the seventh day is already coded with the three letters which comprise Shabbat–שבת. (Exodus 16 and all of this will be discussed in chapter 17, "The *Shabbat* of *Shabbatot*.")

God created the world in six days. Through one breath, He could have formed the world instantly and presented it to us on a silver platter, **but He chose to unfold His creation verbally in a pattern of six days. When we consider the advent of *Shabbat* with the seventh day, the work of creation was finished.** God made order out of chaos on earth and throughout the universe. God did nothing creative on the seventh day.[7]

Logically, once He completed the work, God could have ended the week and limited it to six days. Instead, He added one extra day: "And *Elohim* blessed the seventh day (*Shabbat*), and He sanctified it..." (Genesis 2:3a, Author's translation).[8] Thus, **God made *Shabbat* distinct from every other day**. The first six days, the days of His creation, were called "good" or contained "good" elements, but **only *Shabbat* received God's blessing and sanctification. *Shabbat* was also the time God stopped His work of making order from chaos.**

Evidently, a seven-day week is a genuine, Divine creation. Thus, it is not surprising why Jews identify "seven" as the

---

[7]In a later chapter, we will investigate a significant curiosity from Genesis 2:2: how could God *complete all His work* (מִכָּל־מְלַאכְתּוֹ, *me'kol m'lach'toe*) on the seventh day *and also cease* on the seventh day?

[8]Genesis 2:3 contains the Hebrew words וַיְבָרֶךְ (*va'ye'va'rech*, and He blessed) and וַיְקַדֵּשׁ (*va'ye'kadesh*, and He sanctified). Two related words are "*bra'cha*" and "*ke'du'sha*," which are commonly translated

Divine number of completion. The term *Shabbat* overflows with biblical concepts and is difficult to translate in a few words. **By accepting the *Shabbat* invitation, we acknowledge that this sacred day is unique**. *Shabbat* cannot be conducted on Sunday, Monday, Tuesday, Wednesday, Thursday, or on Friday during the day (more on this later) because our modern weekdays represent the six days God labored to make order from chaos. If we choose to "*Shabbat*" on one of these days, we are effectively transferring a day infused with *sanctification and blessing* and casting it into a day that was *originally dominated by chaos*. As you consider my *Shabbat* invitation, I would like you to ponder what it means to empty yourself completely of the chaos in your week and prepare yourself for whatever God has in store for you in a scheduled meeting with Him.

> *Weekdays are meant for work (the act of bringing chaos into order), but Shabbat is reserved for blessing and sanctification.* ***Chaos and Shabbat should not be mixed!***

---

as "blessing" and "sanctification." Such simple translations bypass important nuances related to creation and to the Sabbath. The words have a unique "God" understanding in Genesis chapter 2 that counters our contemporary human interpretations. The details will astonish you. See chapter 5, "Blessing and Sanctification."

Notes

Chapter 5 Highlights

- God uses familiar (Hebrew) terms in unfamiliar ways throughout Genesis chapter 1.
- The Hebrew word for "light" is "*or,*" but in Genesis chapter 1 it means "linear time."
- "Blessing" in Genesis 2:3 means "the Amplified Presence of God."
- The Bible is not a science or history book. It is a Divine text about the relationship between God and humanity.
- "Past," "present," and "future" are Divine constructs.
- In Genesis 2:1-3, God is creating *Shabbat*. The story of humanity begins in Genesis 2:4.
- *Kadosh*, "sanctification," means "transparency."
- "*Shabbat* transparency" provides us an opportunity to reflect and manifest His purposes in the world.

Your Sabbath Invitation

Blessing and Sanctification

The concepts of "blessing" (*bra'cha*) and "sanctification" (*ke'du'sha*) in Genesis 2:3 are unique and extremely important! When the Scripture says that God blessed and sanctified the seventh day (the Sabbath), the original meaning transcends what we interpret today. My enhanced understanding of these terms was inspired by Dr. Zvi Grumet's book *Genesis: From Creation to Covenant*, where he proposes that God uses familiar Hebrew terms in unfamiliar ways throughout Genesis chapter 1:

> Five words particularly stand out, demanding attention, including some of the words we take most for granted: *or*, *ĥoshekh*, *yom*, *erev*, and *boker*, usually translated, respectively, as "light," "darkness," "day," "evening," and "morning." All these words appear in the opening passage of Genesis, yet it is only after they are used that they are defined,

> indicating that they initially mean something other than what we intuitively assume.[1]

Grumet's proposal is ingenious. I submit that "blessing" (*bra'cha*) and "sanctification" (*ke'du'sha*) possess a "God" understanding in Genesis chapter 1 that diverges from humanity's current understanding of the same words. For example, in our post Genesis chapter 1 world, "darkness" means the absence of light. What do "darkness" and "light" mean in Genesis 1:3–4? Look at both verses in Table 5:

Table 5. Genesis 1:3–4 (Author's translation)

וַיֹּאמֶר אֱלֹהִים יְהִי אוֹר וַיְהִי־אוֹר (*vayomer Elohim y'hi* **or** *vay'hi-***or**) "And *Elohim* said, 'Let it be *or*,' and it was *or*."
וַיַּרְא אֱלֹהִים אֶת־הָאוֹר כִּי־טוֹב וַיַּבְדֵּל אֱלֹהִים בֵּין הָאוֹר וּבֵין הַחֹשֶׁךְ׃ (*vayareh Elohim et-haor kee-tov va'yav'del Elohim bane ha'or oo'bane ha'cho'shech*) "And *Elohim* saw that the *or* is good. And *Elohim* separated between the *or* and between the *ĥoshekh*."

What is transpiring in Table 5? The events in Genesis 1:3–4 occur on the **first day**. When God is creating "light,"

[1] Dr. Zvi Grumet, *Genesis: From Creation to Covenant* (New Milford, CT: Maggid Books, 2017), 25.

He is obviously creating **a light that differs from sunlight** because the sun was not created until the **fourth day**. Therefore, the term "*or*" must have another connotation. Both darkness (*ĥoshekh*) and light (*or*) are separate creations in Genesis chapter 1. However, in our contemporary world, which is post Genesis chapter 1, science defines darkness as the absence of light–not as two distinct entities. So, our understanding of darkness differs from the Divine construct God introduced into the world in Genesis 1. Remember, in Genesis 1, God is creating and separating, producing order out of chaos. On the first day, *or* and *ĥoshekh* were **still intertwined** until they were **later separated** on the **same** first day. In fact, *ĥoshekh* (darkness) was created before *or* (light).

*The light God created on the first day **was not sunlight**. **The sun was created later**, on the fourth day!*

Similarly, we scientifically define a "day" as one twenty-four hour rotation of the earth, yet in Genesis 1:5, 8, and 13–before the earth is fully formed–the term "day" (*yom*) **must** have a **different** meaning. The same logic applies to "evening" (*erev*) and "morning" (*boker*) because they are functions of the rotation of the earth. Their individual positions with respect to the sun determine whether it is daytime or nighttime. Prior

***Prior to a fully-formed earth** with a 24-hour rotation, **"day" has a different meaning**.*

to the creation of the sun, all of these terms **must** have alternative meanings because the sun was not created until Genesis 1:14!

The Bible is not a science or history book. **It is a sacred Divine text about the relationship between God and humanity.** God is an Intelligent, Organized, and Powerful Designer. Genesis chapter 1 is more than a record of objects created by God in the unfolding of the creation story. **The chapter also contains insights on how God is establishing a relationship between Himself and humanity**.

Genesis 1 contains insights on God's relationship with humanity.

Grumet proposes that "*or*" on the first day of creation means "linear time." God–**who is above space and time**– in His grace and mercy, created humanity in a space framed within a Divine construct of **past, present, and future time**. God desired humanity to choose Him **freely**, but He also knew freedom of choice presupposed that human beings could deny and reject Him.

Thankfully, because he is Omniscient, God is also cognizant that some who denied will reconsider their act of rejection and return to faith in Him. Sadly, others may *feel* their past mistakes are too sinful. The emotional and psychological baggage (feelings of shame, regret, and guilt) associated with their previous negative actions is too burdensome. In the end, the lingering baggage often prevents such individuals from reestablishing a relationship with God and moving forward in faith.

Others may choose an abrupt and simpler solution by relinquishing a life with God completely.[2] Again, thankfully, **with the Divine construct of past, present, and future, the individual who says "yes" to God in the present can be separated immediately from the burden of past mistakes** and begin to experience a new **future** with Him.

The past has no bearing on a restored relationship with God after one truly repents. Clearly, **I am not implying that there are no earthly consequences** from certain sinful acts, **but regarding one's innermost relationship with God, the past does not impact the restoration**.

One's past has no impact on their restored relationship with God!

Grumet's book is worth purchasing, if merely to appreciate his keen methodology for defining various Hebrew terms in Genesis chapter 1. Regarding blessing (*bra'cha*) and holy (*kadosh*) in Genesis 2:3, Grumet explains both terms according to the context of Exodus 20:11, the Sabbath mandate delineated in the Ten Commandments (Ten Categorical Statements). **However, I am extending Grumet's statement of "God uses familiar Hebrew terms in unfamiliar ways" to *bra'cha* and *kadosh*!** Thus, my opening premise is: **Genesis 2:1–3 should be included in Genesis 1**, and **Genesis 2:4 initiates the second chapter**. Folks, I determined this nugget according to the context of Genesis 2.

---

[2]"Simpler solution" does not erase the future consequences of severing a relationship with God!

In Genesis 2:1–3, God is creating *Shabbat* and is therefore still addressing the creation story. The story of humanity begins in Genesis 2:4. Also, there are no one-word English translations to define *bra'cha* and *kadosh.* To simply translate *bra'cha* as "blessing" and *kadosh* as "sanctification" omits the nuances and depth in these biblical terms.

> *The creation story continues through Genesis 2:1–3; **God is creating Shabbat!** Genesis 2:4 begins **humanity's story**.*

Some people equate blessing with the concept of permission such as, the classic situation of a man asking his girlfriend's father for the daughter's hand in marriage. The hopeful son-in-law seeks approval while simultaneously praying to receive a "blessing" from his potential father-in-law. Others define blessing in terms of economic prosperity, good health, protection, and the like. For other committed people of faith, blessing has been equated with praise, thankfulness, and benedictions such as, "Grace Before or After Meals." **In Judaism, the introductory template for any liturgical *bra'cha* is "*Baruch Ata Adonai,*" which means "You, God, are the Source of all blessing."** In Genesis 1, the term *bra'cha* occurs twice:

> And He, *Elohim*, blessed (*bra'cha*) them saying, "Be fertile and increase, and fill the waters in the Seas, and let the birds increase on the earth" (Genesis 1:22, Author's translation). And He, *Elohim*, blessed (*bra'cha*) them. And He said to them, "Be

> fertile, and increase, and fill the earth, and master it; and rule over the fish of the sea, the birds of the sky, and all the living creatures that crawl on earth" (Genesis 1:28, Author's translation).

In this context, *bra'cha* is defined as "multiplicity" or "more of." The etymology of *bra'cha* (ברכה) is *bray'cha* (בריכה), which signifies a "water source" in Mishnaic Hebrew, similar to a cistern. In Genesis 2:3, God does not provide the wording of the *bra'cha*, indicating that the *bra'cha* is created for another purpose. Therefore, one can aptly conclude that **God created the concept of *Shabbat bra'cha* for His purposes, in order to serve His intentions concerning His relationship with humanity. God created a day where humanity can experience His Amplified Presence in order to connect intimately and more intensely to the ultimate Source– God Himself**.

Bra'cha is "multiplicity" or "more of."

The word *kadosh* is first introduced to us in Genesis 2:3. Some translate the term as "holy," "designated," or "separate." **I prefer to use the Rabbi Manis Friedman's translation of *kadosh* as "transparency."**[3]

Kadosh is "transparency."

---

[3]Manis Friedman, "What is 'Holiness'?", Dean of Bais Chana Women's Institute of Jewish Studies, interview by Michael Chighel, n.d., Chabad.org, n.d., n.p., https://www.chabad.org/multimedia/mediacdo/aid/676159/jewish/What-Is-Holiness.htm/ (1 July 2021).

The world has a Creator, and He has a purpose, but the creation does not always allow the Creator to manifest His purpose. The world lacks the transparency Rabbi Friedman described. **When we apply this idea to the seventh day, we understand that God created *Shabbat kodesh–Shabbat* transparency–to allow God and His purpose to become visible in the world.**

Shabbat kodesh was created to allow God and His purpose to become visible in the world.

Transparency only occurs after the *bra'cha* establishes God's Amplified Presence. The other days of the week, based on chaos becoming order, hinder the Amplified Presence, the transparency of God, and His purpose. The Amplified Presence or the *bra'cha* is only manifested on a day that is completely ordered and without chaos. Thus, every *Shabbat* is an opportunity to reflect on the transparency of the day in order to become more transparent in our own lives, **to make His purpose more visible in the world for the upcoming week**.

Notes

PART TWO

A day for God's mercy

Chapter 6 Highlights

- God could have eradicated Adam and Eve for their sins. Instead, He allowed humanity to live.
- The revelation that God is merciful originated with Adam on *Shabbat*.
- *Shabbat* is the conduit for God's original merciful act.
- Psalms are songs with lyrics and melodies. Psalm titles unlock a Psalm's meaning.
- The Book of Psalms is the soul of Scripture and the Bible's original hymnbook.
- In the Hebrew Bible, superscriptions (titles) are Scripture.
- Revelations can be "mined" from superscriptions in the same way they are mined from other Scripture.
- Psalm 92 is the only psalm designated to a day—the Sabbath (*Shabbat*). The Levites sang Psalm 92 on *Shabbat*.

Your Sabbath Invitation

God's Original Merciful Act

So far in *Your Sabbath Invitation*, I have discussed several topics and provided study tools related to *Shabbat*: the End-Time prophecy in Isaiah 66; mining or decoding revelation from the Bible using the Hebrew language; exegesis and hermeneutics; and appointed times. You learned that Sabbath is a process, and "now" is an ideal time to integrate the process into your life. *Shabbat* is a special celebration that cannot be transferred to a weekday. You also discovered that the six weekdays were conceived in chaos, but God eliminated chaos by the seventh day. In addition, the *Shabbat* was the only day God sanctified. Lastly and hopefully, I have sparked a desire within you to esteem the Sabbath invitation.

After Adam and Eve partook of the fruit from the Tree of Knowledge of Good and Evil, God could have eradicated humanity immediately. No one would exist today. **Instead, by His infinite mercy, God allowed humanity to live. The**

revelation that God is merciful originated with Adam, and this revelation occurred on *Shabbat*.

> ***Shabbat* is the conduit** *for the original, merciful act of God.*

To prepare for the scriptural expedition ahead, which links *Shabbat* to God's original merciful act, please consider the following points:

1. Psalms are songs, which means every psalm possessed an original melody.
2. Psalm titles are extremely important. Often, they are the keys for unlocking the theology of the sacred text.
3. The title for Psalm 92 begins with the rare Hebrew expression, *Mizmor Shir*, which English Bibles translate incorrectly.
4. Psalm 92 is the oldest psalm, and Adam is its author.
5. King David is not the only author of the Psalms.
6. Remember, Hebrew is written and read from right to left.

Connecting Shabbat and God's Mercy

The first time I heard the teaching about *Shabbat* and God's merciful act I was probably nine years old. I was stunned. I always understood why God sent Adam and Eve (חַוָּה, *Chavah*, in Hebrew) from the Garden of Eden—both of them had violated God's direct orders.[1] However, I did not comprehend, until much later in life, that God's mercy delivered Adam, Eve (*Chavah*), and every human being from total destruction. More than that, humanity's unmerited rescue occurred on *Shabbat*.

*The Book of Psalms is the **soul of Scripture** and **the Bible's original hymnbook**. All of the Psalms have **melodies!***

There are five main points that correlate *Shabbat* and God's merciful act. We will address two points in this chapter and the last three in subsequent chapters. The first point concerns melodies. **The Book of Psalms is not only the soul of Scripture, it is also the Bible's original hymnbook**. Technically, the words and testimonies contained in our 150 Psalms are lyrics, which articulate every human emotion, including joy, fear, depression, triumph, and ecstasy. The lyrics signify that the *Ruach Hakodesh* (Holy Spirit) rested on every composer and singer.

During the Second Temple Period (516 BCE–70 CE), on a daily basis, the Levites sang from the Psalms in the Temple. Psalms were designated for each day. For example, on the fourth day (Wednesday), the Levites sang Psalm 94. Their musical deliveries engaged the hearers and deepened the people's reception and comprehension of the Psalms. The Levites were not reciting; they were singing!

---

[1]Read the discussion of *Chavah* in Appendix A-2, "*Adom* and *Ha'Adom*."

Although we have the lyrics from the Psalms, their original melodies are lost. However, with a little imagination an individual could be inspired to compose his or her own melodies. Envision the following: a psalmist with training in ancient music travels to the southern steps of the Temple Mount. While climbing the stairs, the psalmist sings the psalm for that day, trying to sense the musical rhythms and breaks the Levites *might have experienced* when they ascended the same Temple steps. Suddenly, the psalmist conceives an amazing melody! The result is not the original, but perhaps it brings the psalmist a "step" closer to what the Levites experienced (pun intended).

The seven Levitical psalms for the seven days are listed in Table 6.

Table 6. Psalms Sung by the Levites Each Day of the Week[2]

Sunday	**Psalm 24**	Access to God's mountaintop
Monday	**Psalm 48**	The security of Jerusalem
Tuesday	**Psalm 82**	God is in the midst of those marginalized by society
Wednesday	**Psalm 94**	A call for God's vengeance on the wicked
Thursday	**Psalm 81**	A plea for national introspection and repentance
Friday	**Psalm 93**	Praising God's Kingship over the world
Saturday	**Psalm 92**	Praising God for His original act of mercy

[2]The daily Psalms are still recited in Jewish morning prayers.

To a large extent, we could characterize the information in Table 6 as the Levites' ancient "playlist." Notice the distinct subjects on the list. There are 150 psalms. Why were these seven selected? The subjects start with the glory of God and conclude with the mercy of God. Each day describes an aspect of God, His kingdom, His ways, His love for Israel, and His justice.

With an understanding that psalms are songs comprised of lyrics and melodies, we can move forward to our chapter's second point: Psalm titles are extremely important because they unlock the theology of the sacred text. Psalm titles are headings that appear beneath the psalm's designated number. Almost 120 of the 150 psalms contain "titles," and scholars refer to them as "superscriptions." Examine Figure 1 below:

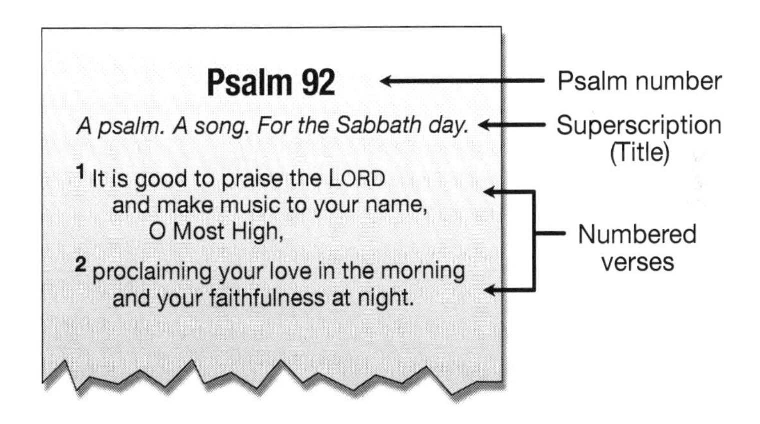

Figure 1. Typical Layout of Psalm 92 in English Bibles

The layout of the Psalm 92 text is similar to that found in the NIV® (2011). The superscription is the next line below the Psalm number. Notice that the superscription appears to be independent of the rest of the psalm. Most printed copies of English Bibles use a similar layout.[3] Secondly, the typeface is smaller than the numbered verses. Finally, the superscription lacks a number, so Psalm 92:1 begins with, "It is good to praise the LORD and make music to your name, O Most High…."[4] If one or more of the formatting styles is combined, they may give the impression that the superscription is not Scripture. In fact, one might hastily conclude that all superscriptions are not Scripture.[5] The issue is more pronounced in Internet versions of the Bible.[6]

Psalm titles are Scripture *and not independent of the Psalm!*

Overall, the Hebrew Bible foregoes superscriptions. **Every phrase and verse in the Psalms has a number and is regarded as Scripture.** For example, Psalm 92:1 in the Jewish Publication Society (JPS) 1917 Bible says, "A Psalm, a Song. For the Sabbath day," while Psalm 92:2 reads, "It is a good thing to give thanks unto the LORD, And to

---

[3]Italics, bold typeface, smaller fonts using the sentence case, or smaller fonts using the upper case are other formatting styles.

[4]For multiple online examples of how superscriptions are presented in over fifty Bibles, visit BibleGateway.com.

[5]Superscriptions are a major debate among Bible scholars. Further discussion about the origin and purpose of superscriptions occurs in chapter 6. Scholarly articles and dissertations pertaining to superscriptions in the Psalms are easily accessible on the Internet.

[6]Over fifty English versions are available on BibleGateway.com.

sing praises unto Thy name, O Most High...." The difference will be more apparent when we compare Figure 1 (page 59) to Figure 2, a layout of the beginning of Psalm 92 similar to the 1917 JPS *Tanakh* (Hebrew Bible).

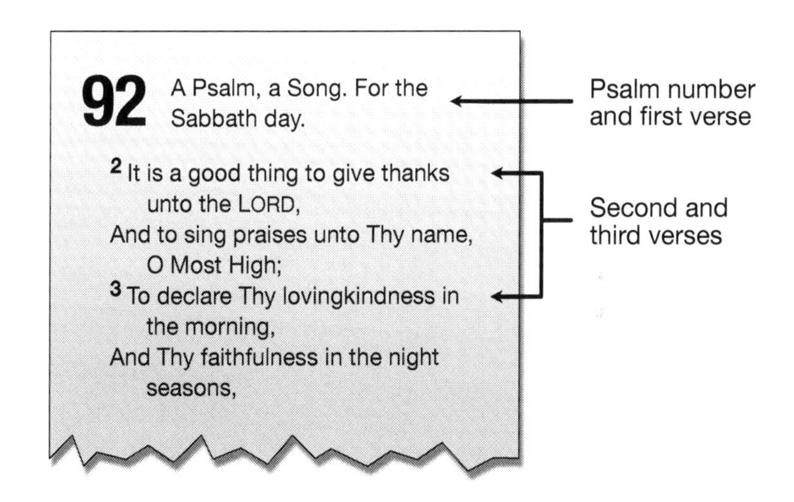

Figure 2. Typical Layout of Psalm 92 in Hebrew Bibles

Below is a sample list of other superscriptions from the Book of Psalms. (Remember, over seventy-five percent of the psalms in most English Bibles have superscriptions.)

1. A psalm of David
2. A prayer of David
3. A *michtam* of David
4. A meditation of David
5. To the Chief Musician

The wording for superscriptions varies. Some superscriptions identify the psalm's author (1 and 2 above). Others include musical terms or provide specific information for the psalm's leader (5). Perhaps superscriptions containing unfamiliar musical expressions will be less puzzling because you now understand that every psalm is a hymn.

Why have I extended this discussion? **We can only mine revelation from Scriptures. If the superscriptions are not Scriptures, they cannot be mined.** Let me assure you, I am not forcing the superscriptions into Scriptures in order to mine them! Rather, I am adhering to the principle I introduced in chapter 2: every word in Torah is from God. Furthermore, who would include the phrase "For the Sabbath," as a title for Psalm 92, when the Psalm mentions nothing about *Shabbat*?

At this point, let me give you a short assignment: marinate, skim, and recognize. Please take a moment to "**marinate**" yourself in this concept: **The superscriptions in the Book of Psalms are Scriptures.** Then, **skim** through the Psalms, choose a few, and **recognize** how much the concept affects your understanding of each psalm. I hope you are captivated and refreshed!

You finished that assignment, now reread the NIV excerpt for Psalm 92. The superscription says, "A psalm. A song. For the Sabbath day." Psalm 92 is the **only** psalm designated to a day–the Sabbath. Finally, review Table 6 (page 58) and uncover this nugget: the Levites sang Psalm 92 on Saturday–the seventh day–because the psalm was designated for the Sabbath (*Shabbat*). Congratulations! We just proved the superscription in Psalm 92 reveals that **the Sabbath is the**

theology for the psalm. In the next chapter, we will discuss why Psalm 92–a sacred text–was designated as the Sabbath psalm, though seemingly, the rest of the psalm lacks any *Shabbat* concepts.

Notes

Chapter 7 Highlights

- Although Psalm 92 is dedicated to the Sabbath, it contains nothing related to the Sabbath.
- The beginning of Psalm 92 uses the Hebrew words *mizmor* and *shir*. Both words are commonly translated as “song.”
- A *mizmor* is an emotionally charged, wordless melody. A *shir* results from contemplation and contains words, rhymes, or poetry.
- A *mizmor shir* is a song initiated by the emotions.
- A *shir mizmor* is a song prompted by the intellect.
- Only two psalms begin with *mizmor shir*, Psalm 92 and Psalm 30.
- The use of *shir mizmor* is also rare.
- *Mizmor shir* and *shir mizmor* are always accompanied by human characters—except in Psalm 92. How can a day be a character?

Your Sabbath Invitation

Lyrics and Melodies

In the last chapter, we learned that psalm titles are Scriptures in the Hebrew Bible, and Psalm 92 is designated as the Sabbath psalm. Yet, when we study the Psalm more closely, we uncover nothing related to the Sabbath. Instead, the psalm articulates praise and worship to God, accounts the downfall of the wicked, and highlights the flourishing of the righteous. Oddly, the only psalm in the Hebrew Bible canon that is dedicated to the Sabbath day lacks any theological or religious teachings about the Sabbath. To appreciate the true connection between the first verse of Psalm 92 and the rest of the psalm, we must examine the Hebrew text.

Psalm 92 begins with **מִזְמוֹר שִׁיר לְיוֹם הַשַּׁבָּת** (*Mizmor Shir L'yom HaShabbat*), translated literally as, "Song, song for the Sabbath day." The words *mizmor* (מִזְמוֹר) and *shir* (שִׁיר) both mean song. **A *mizmor* is a sincere, emotionally charged, wordless melody.** It originates from the soul, not the intellect. **A *shir* is a different kind of song because it**

***does* emerge from the intellect.** A *shir* is a product of contemplation, consideration, and language. Its final form always contains words, rhymes, or poetry.[1]

Typically, when artists compose songs, either the lyrics or the words develop first. It is rare for the lyrics and the melody to emerge, fully developed, at the same time.[2] Even the Bible acknowledges the rarity. When a songwriter or psalmist **simultaneously conceives melody and lyrics**, the action is expressed using the Hebrew terms ***mizmor* and *shir***. In the Book of Psalms, the words are combined and two terms result: *mizmor shir* or *shir mizmor*. If we apply the definitions above, a *mizmor shir* describes a song initiated by the emotions, and a *shir mizmor* is a song prompted by the intellect.

Mizmor shir and *shir mizmor* are used when melody and lyrics emerge simultaneously.

Seldom does a psalm open with the words *mizmor shir* or *shir mizmor*. In fact, there are only two psalms that begin with *mizmor shir* (מִזְמוֹר שִׁיר). Look at Table 7 on the following page:

---

[1]See Chanan Morrison, "Psalm 30: Mizmor Shir-Melody and Song," Ravkook torah.org, 2019, n.p., http://www.ravkooktorah.org/PSALM30.htm/ (3 March 2021).

[2]See the great interview of Paul Simon describing how he wrote *Bridge Over Troubled Waters*, The Dick Cavett Show, "Paul Simon On His Writing Process for 'Bridge Over Troubled Water,'" The Dick Cavett Show, YouTube video, 10:45, Jan 27, 2020, https://www.youtube.com/watch?v=qFt0cP-klQI. Fast-forward to the 6:22–9:53 minute mark. Simon did not compose his former number one song in thirty minutes!

Table 7. The *Mizmor Shir* Begins the Psalm

Mizmor Shir Dedication of the house to David	**Psalm 30**
Mizmor Shir to the Sabbath Day	**Psalm 92**

The term is effective in both Psalms; we will examine their impact in chapter 11. In Table 8, notice that *mizmor shir* appears later in the first verse of three other psalms:

Table 8. The *Mizmor Shir* Appears Later in the Psalm

For the Chief Musician; with stringed instruments ***mizmor shir*** **:** …	**Psalm 67**
For the Chief Musician to David ***mizmor shir*** **:** …	**Psalm 68**
To the sons of Korah ***mizmor shir*** his foundation in the holy mountains (Author's translation)	**Psalm 87**

The ***mizmor shir*** **is scarce in the Scriptures**, but it certainly has *verse position* flexibility. In Psalms 67 and 68 above, notice that the *mizmor shirim* (plural of *shir*) occur after the main characters in the verse. In Table 9, the unique expression is now reversed to שִׁיר מִזְמוֹר (shir *mizmor*):

Table 9. The *Shir Mizmor* Begins the Psalm

Shir mizmor to the children of Korah**:** …	**Psalm 48**
Shir mizmor to Asaph**:** …	**Psalm 83**
Shir mizmor to the children of Korah…	**Psalm 88**

The *shir mizmor*, like the *mizmor shir*, can initiate a verse. Glance at Psalms 48 and 83. Then glance back at Psalms 67 and 68. What differences and similarities do you see? Are you more convinced how important it is to regard the Psalms as songs? Lastly, in Table 10 the *shir mizmor* in Psalm 66 appears in the middle of the verse:

Table 10. The *Shir Mizmor* Occurs Later in the Psalm

For the Chief Musician. ***Shir mizmor.*** Shout with joy to God; all the earth.	**Psalm 66**

There are three grammatical periods in the English translation of Psalm 66, but there are no periods in the Hebrew text.

How are you doing? Are you ready to end chapter 7? If so, review Tables 7 thru 10 once more and observe the following: **in every Psalm, each *mizmor shir* and *shir mizmor* is accompanied by a human character** such as, the Chief Musician, sons of Korah, or Asaph–**except Psalm 92**. **The character joining the *mizmor shir* in Psalm 92 is the Sabbath.** How can a day be a character? We will answer this question in the next chapter.

The character *accompanying the mizmor shir in Psalm 92* ***is the Sabbath****.*

Notes

Chapter 8 Highlights

- "Tradition" establishes Adam as the author of Psalm 92. Here, tradition means "*midrash*."
- The Hebrew term "*midrash*" comes from the verb "*dra'sh*," "to seek." We seek God when we expound Scripture and apply revelations to everyday life.
- The noun "*midrash*" refers to the *process* of seeking biblical revelations. It also refers to the *revelation* received.
- The proper noun "*Midrash*" is a compilation of biblical revelations.
- *Midrash* is authoritative Jewish commentary, composed as far back as the Second Temple Period (516 BCE–70 CE).
- One example of *midrash* identifies a fig, not an apple, as the *forbidden fruit* eaten by Adam and Eve (*Chavah*).
- *Midrash* is for elucidation, but not every *midrash* is simple to understand.

Your Sabbath Invitation

Dra'shing

Praise God for lyrics, songs, and titles in the Hebrew Bible! Now you comprehend that a psalm is a song, and psalm titles (superscriptions) are part of canonized Scripture, not simple chapter headings. You learned two Hebrew words–*mizmor* and *shir.* A *mizmor* is a song where the melody emerges first, prompted by an emotional experience the songwriter has endured. A *shir* is a song where the lyrics proceed first, after a thoughtful revelation from the composer. It is extremely uncommon for a *mizmor shir* or *shir mizmor* combination to occur in the Book of Psalms and almost unheard of for either one to open a Psalm. Psalm 92 opens with the *mizmor shir* combination.

> *Rarely does a mizmor shir or shir mizmor open a Psalm.*

In earlier discussions, I stated that Adam composed Psalm 92, establishing him as one of several songwriters of the Book of Psalms. After reviewing Psalm 92, are you now wondering, "David, why are you attributing authorship to Adam because the Psalm never mentions his name? In fact, Psalm 92 does not mention any biblical characters." Your point is valid and my succinct response is "Tradition!" What do I mean by tradition? With respect to *Your Sabbath Invitation*, the word tradition means "*midrash*!"

The Amazing World of Midrash

For a number of you reading *Your Sabbath Invitation*, the word *midrash* is completely foreign. Is it a Jewish term? Is it related to the Bible or to hermeneutics? Is *midrash* an action or a *traditional* way of thinking? The answer is "Yes, yes, and yes!" The term *midrash*, like many Hebrew words, cannot be defined by one English word. The expression *midrash* stems from the Hebrew root word "דרש" (*dra'sh*), which means "to seek." **When applied to Bible study, to "*dra'sh*" is to seek God by expounding every corner and facet of a Scripture.** Scripture is intended to be read and expounded![1] Ultimately, the goal of *midrash* is to unravel the deeper meaning of the sacred text, and at times, to apply the resulting revelations to everyday life. **The word *midrash*, a noun, is *the process* of seeking biblical revelations. The revelation that one obtains from the**

> ***Dra'sh*** *is a verb which means to seek or excavate biblical texts.*

[1]Babylonian Talmud Kiddushin 49a.

process is also called "*midrash*." The plural of *midrash* is *midrashim*.

When *midrash* occurs as the proper noun "*Midrash*," it usually refers to a *compilation* of biblical revelations. Basically, our "*Midrash*" is **authoritative** Jewish commentary–an accepted body of historic rabbinic revelations, which have been in the process of being composed as far back as the end of the Second Temple Period (516 BCE–70 CE). Rabbis attained revelations through meticulous examinations of the Scriptures and lively rabbinic debates. *Midrash* is one of the most interesting, important, and complex elements in Jewish biblical literature. Expect many lively encounters with *midrash* throughout *Your Sabbath Invitation*.

Shortly, you will discover that I not only discuss numerous *midrashim* (plural of *midrash*), but I also ***dra'sh*** several *midrashim* and even ***dra'sh*** the biblical text myself! Yes, it is possible for trained individuals to ***dra'sh*** the Hebrew Bible for personal applications or Bible studies because only specific rabbinic *midrashim* are considered authoritative![2]

One example of *midrash* attempts to identify the fruit Adam and Eve (*Chavah*) ate in the Garden of Eden. Genesis 2:17 says, "but you must not eat from the tree of the knowledge of good and evil, for when you eat from it you will certainly die." Genesis 3:6a reads, "When the woman saw that the fruit of the tree was good…, she took some and ate it."

---

[2]For a deeper understanding of *midrash*, consult Appendix A-1, "The Essentials of *midrash* and *Midrash*."

I am certain most of you have heard or been taught that the fruit was an apple. However, the word "apple" is not mentioned in any English Bible translation.[3] Likewise, the Hebrew word for apple is absent from the Hebrew biblical text. Several theories explain how the *forbidden fruit* became an apple. The most recognized theory is too complex to discuss here. It involves a detailed analysis of Genesis 2:17; 3:5–6; Proverbs 25:11; and the linguistic choices Jerome implemented for his Latin Vulgate.[4]

Briefly, the Latin word for evil in Genesis 2:17–*mali* (pronounced *măli*)–was confused with the Latin word for apples in Proverbs 25:11–*mala* (pronounced *māla*). Twelve centuries after Jerome finished the Vulgate (from the sixteenth century CE and forward), artists and writers intermingled various language and cultural similarities between *mali* and *mala* and devised many *forbidden fruit* theories. **Ultimately, the apple emerged as the "fruit" that Eve (*Chavah*) and Adam ate in Genesis 3:6**.

Over the centuries, the Latin for "evil" became confused with the Latin for "apples."

If we examine the original Hebrew text, which is the best approach (Jerome translated the Bible from Hebrew texts, not Latin manuscripts!), we will discover that the Hebrew words for "evil" and "apple" are completely unrelated. In Genesis 2:17 and 3:5, the Hebrew word for evil is "רע"

---

[3]See https://www.biblegateway.com/verse/en/Genesis%202:17/ (1 February 2022) for fifty-four Bible versions and translations.

[4]Jerome translated the Hebrew Bible into Latin in the fourth century CE.

(*ra*) while the Hebrew word for apples in Proverbs 25:11 is "תפוחי" (*ta'pu'cheh*). **Both words are linguistically and visibly unrelated.** So, according to the Hebrew text, it is impossible to identify the apple as the *forbidden fruit*. Now, in view of the Hebrew linguistics, does the Bible specify or allude to another fruit for Genesis 3:6? Of course!

> According to a *midrash* for Genesis 3, ***the forbidden fruit was a fig!***

Talmidim (students), we will disregard the apple theories and conduct a Hebraic study of a *midrash* for Genesis 3. **This particular *midrash*–from the larger body of *midrashim*–claims the fruit was a fig.** The fig theory is based on Genesis 3:7, where Adam and Eve (*Chavah*) clothed themselves with fig leaves. **This theory presumes that the tree that helped Adam and Eve had to be an accessory to the crime. Elementary, *talmidim*!** The Genesis 3 *midrash* is clear and reasonable.

At this point, you just experienced your first *midrash*! Let me congratulate you! While the goal of *midrash* is elucidation and biblical revelation, not every *midrash* is as simple as the one for Genesis 3. If you rewind back to the main question for this chapter: "How is Adam the author of the Psalm when Psalm 92 never mentions his name?", you will recall that my breezy answer was "*midrash*!" In the next chapter we will answer this question by examining an elaborate *midrash* for Psalm 92.[5]

---

[5]If you need additional preparation for the excavation in chapter 9, please read "The Goals of *Midrash*" portion in Appendix A-1.

Notes

Chapter 9 Highlights

- The word *midrash* also refers to biblical revelations obtained from *dra'shing*.
- Rabbinic *midrashim* are an indispensable source for advanced Bible study.
- *Midrash* often answers the questions you should have asked. Orthodox Jews draw closer to God by asking the right questions.
- Prepositions are extremely important in *midrash*. Psalm 92 is dedicated "to" *Shabbat*.
- Humanity and *Shabbat* are the main characters in Psalm 92.
- For his sin, Adam should have obtained immediate death. Instead, he received infinite mercy from God.
- Metaphorically, *Shabbat* became Adam's defense attorney.
- Adam composed Psalm 92 the day after he sinned because he received a new lease on life.

Your Sabbath Invitation

Adam's Defense Attorney

idrash is an essential interpretive tool in *Your Sabbath Invitation*, and most of you have just experienced your first technical encounter with *midrash*. Concisely, *midrash*: 1) is a way of probing the text of the Hebrew Scriptures. Through the process, individuals receive revelation; 2) offers intense engagements with God's Word; 3) provides novel insights into the Hebrew Bible; and 4) is a primary means for establishing a deeper relationship with God. The Hebrew verb *dra'sh* describes the process because the term means to "seek." **The word *midrash* also refers to the biblical revelations we obtain from *dra'shing*.** The proper noun, *Midrashim*, is an authoritative Jewish commentary, which contains thousands of rabbinic biblical revelations. Portions of the *midrashim* date as far back as the close of the Second Temple Period.

> *The word **midrash** includes biblical revelations obtained from **dra'shing** (seeking).*

From the start, I tried to avoid *midrash* in *Your Sabbath Invitation.* **Rabbinic *midrashim* are an indispensable source for advanced Bible study; the revelations are creative and instructive.** On the other hand, *midrashim* are also highly interwoven and difficult to summarize. Above all, the most challenging task is ascertaining how the rabbis reached their conclusions! To my surprise, *Your Sabbath Invitation* steadily demanded–even yearned for–the layered insights the *midrashim* offer. One demand was the unanswered question from the previous chapter: "How is Adam the author of the Psalm when Psalm 92 never mentions his name?" My swift response was "*midrash*!" My current response is, "We will answer the riddle by *dra'shing* an elaborate *midrash* on Psalm 92."

To ***dra'sh*** like an expert, let me equip you with an *essential* operative phrase: ***midrash* often answers the questions you should have asked.** Revelations and statements in our canonized *midrashim* are based on myriad questions that beloved rabbis have asked throughout the centuries. The *midrashim* may or may not contain the exact questions from our rabbis, but *the resulting revelations prove that the questions were asked.* **As Orthodox Jews, we learn by asking questions; we study the Bible by asking questions; we obtain revelation by asking questions; we get closer to God by asking the right questions.**

> *Midrash* often answers the questions **you should have asked!**

Dear readers, your training period for the new "operative phrase" just ended. The next tour on your journey commences with three questions and a *midrash*! Are you ready? The *midrash* concerns Psalm 92, which grapples with the following: 1) **Why does Psalm 92 specify the Sabbath?**; 2) **Why is the Psalm dedicated to the Sabbath Day?**; and 3) **Why did the composer write *l'yom HaShabbat*, "to the Sabbath Day," as opposed to *b'yom HaShabbat*, "on the Sabbath Day"?** (In *midrash*, prepositions are *extremely* important.)[1] For convenience, we can trim these questions to "Why ***specify***?"; "Why ***dedicate***?"; and "Why ***l'yom***?" My answers and explanation are based on the *midrash.*[2]

Firstly, remember that Psalm 92:1 reads, *Mizmor shir l'yom HaShabbat*, "Song, song for the Sabbath Day" or "Song, song for the *Shabbat* Day" (Author's translation). Secondly, notice that the writer chose *l'yom* instead of *b'yom.* The preposition in *l'yom* is "to." The "to" indicates that the writer is **dedicating and paying homage to** someone or something. The obvious recipient is the *Shabbat* Day (Sabbath Day). Thirdly, the rabbis restricted the Psalm's context to sacred history.[3] So, the two subjects,

---

[1]As you just discovered, from antiquity, rabbis have taught and learned by asking questions. You observe the same method whenever you read Matthew, Mark, Luke, and John! Rabbinic questions tackle multiple puzzles related to word choices, omitted words and letters, word repetition, wordplays, and the like.

[2]*Bereishit Rabbah* 22:13, *Sefaria.org*, n.p., https://www.sefaria.org.il/Psalms.92?with=Midrash&lang=bi/ (8 July 2021).

[3]The term "sacred history" refers to the biblical events that transpired in Genesis 1-3.

> *Humanity and Shabbat are the main characters in Psalm 92, and Adam is the psalm's author.*

humanity and *Shabbat*, function metaphorically as the **main characters** in Psalm 92. The psalmist represents humanity, and *Shabbat* is the masterpiece in God's creation. Finally, **the rabbis concluded that Adam authored Psalm 92 as a dedication to *Shabbat*.**

With the proposition that Adam composed Psalm 92 and that the Psalm is dedicated to the Sabbath Day, we can begin to unpack the meaning of the psalm. In Genesis 2:17, God warned Adam of the deathly consequences of eating from [the] Tree of the Knowledge of Good and Evil, "but you must not eat from the tree of the knowledge of good and evil, for when you eat from it you will certainly die." **In Hebrew, the death consequences are expressed more severely with the use of two words that relate to death "מוֹת תָּמוּת"** (*mot tamut*, you will **certainly die**). After Adam partook of fruit from [the] Tree of the Knowledge of Good and Evil (3:6), imagine his mindset. Undoubtedly, Adam is contemplating the graveyard as his next destination, but he does not die. **Adam is a "dead man walking"!**

Although Adam lacked any visual or tangible experiences with death, he obviously understood death's implications. Presumably, God had already explained the meaning of death to Adam or to Eve (*Chavah*) because the couple hid from God's presence immediately after their transgression (Gen 3:8).

When we read the Garden of Eden episode in Genesis chapter 3, the narrative omits a specific date or time. Scripturally speaking, we only know the incident occurred sometime after Adam and Eve (*Chavah*) were created. Therefore, from the knowledge that Adam composed Psalm 92 and that he dedicated it to the Sabbath Day, I infer that the Garden of Eden event transpired **prior** to a Sabbath. **If this is true, I maintain that Adam's sin occurred on a Friday**, which the Bible calls the sixth day. (Remember, the Sabbath Day begins every Friday at sunset, not at 12:00 am on Saturday!)

> *Adam and Eve (Chavah) sinned on a Friday, just prior to a Sabbath.*

On the other hand, could I propose Tuesday or Wednesday as the day for Adam's sin (the third and fourth days of the week)? My definitive answer is "No." If Adam had sinned on Tuesday, the third day, then the superscription of Psalm 92 would have read: "A psalm. For the Fourth day." This is a crucial point; let me explain.

Strict justice demands instantaneous retribution. Adam consciously disobeyed a direct order from God; he was not delirious, confused, or ill. God is the Judge and Jury, and His verdict was perfectly clear in Genesis 2:17. Adam should have received **immediate** physical death, instead, he obtained undeserved, infinite mercy from God. Adam did not die! Adam's response was gracious and conveyed musically via Psalm 92.

> *Strict justice demands instantaneous retribution.*

In Psalm 92:1, we find a *mizmor shir* and the dedication to the Sabbath. For a moment, recall the definition and function of a *mizmor shir*: an instantaneous transfer of emotion and intellect, which follows a traumatic life event and manifests as a song. Seemingly, the Sabbath becomes Adam's primary **defense** against instantaneous retribution from God on Friday. ***Shabbat* is Adam's defense attorney, the personified (metaphorical) main character of Psalm 92.**

By writing Psalm 92 and dedicating it "to the Sabbath Day" (*l'yom HaShabbat*), **Adam declares to God that judgment cannot be executed on a day that He, God, had previously made holy** (Genesis 2:3). Instead of receiving immediate physical death on Friday or on *Shabbat*, Adam received mercy from God. The devastating event for Adam was his sin, but the next day, **he witnessed the power of the Sabbath and experienced God's mercy on the Sabbath**. After receiving a new lease on life, **the day *after* he sinned, Adam composed Psalm 92. God is the Merciful One, not the Judge and Jury alone.** In the next chapter, we will dive a bit deeper into Adam's process for discovering that God is merciful.

Adam wrote Psalm 92 in response to God's mercy and the power of Shabbat.

Notes

Chapter 10 Highlights

- Adam was created from the standpoint of strict justice. Only later did he experience mercy.
- Hebrew names of God are intentional, descriptive, and prophetic.
- The name *Elohim* means "All Powerful." *Elohim* is used 35 times in Genesis 1:1-2:3.
- You will not find the expression "that *it was* good" on the second day of creation.
- The Tetragrammaton, "The Eternal," represents God's Attribute of Mercy. Mercy tempers Strict Justice.
- Only humanity is authorized to function with free will.
- When God rescued Adam, He also rescued all of humanity. Psalm 92 is Adam's response to God's original act of mercy.
- The Sabbath invitation is a pipeline to Adam, who was freed from temporary life support to continue an intimate life with God.

Your Sabbath Invitation

Freed From Temporary Life Support

reedom for an incarcerated person is an indispensable gift and desire, but it is often costly. To ensure a victorious trial and to avoid potential imprisonment, defendants frequently pay attorneys exorbitant fees to defend them in court. In extreme contrast, without spending a dollar, Adam obtained freedom from immediate death–for himself and for humanity–through the infinite mercy of God. Adam's attorney was the Sabbath, and the court's record of his confession is Psalm 92.

Earlier, I presented Adam as the author of Psalm 92. After studying the psalm's background, we learned that a reversal of Adam's dire situation inspired the psalm. In his current predicament, **Adam only knew God from the standpoint of strict justice.** When God spared Adam after he ate the fruit from "[the] Tree of Knowledge of Good and Evil," he realized that God is also merciful.

God created Adam from the standpoint of strict justice!

Instead of death, God allowed Adam to continue living. The epiphany of Adam's internal understanding that God is merciful occurred on the Sabbath.

You may be asking why did Adam originally view God through the perspective of strict justice? **The answer is *Elohim*, one of the names of God that means "All Powerful" and one that represents His Attribute of Strict Justice.** The Bible opens with the narrative of creation using the name of *Elohim*. In fact, the name *Elohim* is used thirty-two times in Genesis chapter 1 and an additional three times in Genesis 2:1–3. The power source of every aspect of creation and its continual existence is sourced in the name of *Elohim*. Table 11 includes every verse that mentions *Elohim* from Genesis 1 through Genesis 2:1–3.

Table 11. 35 References to *Elohim* (אֱלֹהִים) in Genesis 1:1–2:3

Genesis 1:1–31	**v. 10 (twice)**	**v. 25 (twice)**
	v. 11	**v. 26**
v. 1	**v. 12**	**v. 27 (twice)**
v. 2	**v. 14**	**v. 28 (twice)**
v. 3	**v. 16**	**v. 29**
v. 4 (twice)	**v. 17**	**v. 31**
v. 5	**v. 18**	
v. 6	**v. 20**	**Genesis 2:1–3**
v. 7	**v. 21 (twice)**	
v. 8	**v. 22**	**v. 2**
v. 9	**v. 24**	**v. 3 (twice)**

Elohim controls the action in the creation account. The name *Elohim* is mentioned thirty-five times in a span of thirty-four verses. Table 11 indicates that six verses acknowledge *Elohim* twice. The Genesis passages are indisputable and clear: *Elohim* is the "All Powerful" Creator. On the other hand, the notion that the name *Elohim* represents God's Attribute of Justice requires greater investigation. **The concept is derived from the judgments God made when He discerned "that *it was* good" (*ki tov*) on *most* but *not on all* of the days of creation.** How many of you noticed that God did **not discern** "that *it was* good" on the second day of creation?[1] Compare Genesis 1:6–8 and Genesis 1:10–13. You will not find "that *it was* good" for the second day (Genesis 1:6–8). However, on the third day of creation, *Elohim* evaluates **twice** "that *it was* good" (Genesis 1:10–13).[2] Readers, this is not a minor oversight or a mistake.

> *The concept of Elohim as God's Attribute of Strict Justice is derived from His judgments "that it was good."*

The second day of creation omits the expression "that *it was* good" because the separation of the lower waters **on the second day** was not yet assigned to the Seas. To rephrase, **a value judgment of "כִּי־טוֹב"** (*ki tov*, that *it was* good, Author's translation) **could not be declared in Scripture until the work was complete**. I imagine that at least half of you raised your hands. "David, is this another

---

[1]Here is an interesting fact. In Genesis 1:10, 12, 18, 21, 25 the Hebrew text says, וַיַּרְא אֱלֹהִים כִּי־טוֹב, "and *Elohim* **discerned** that *it was* good," (Author's translation), not "and *Elohim* **said** that *it was* good." God's judgments were **discerning**, not verbal!

[2]Shlomo Yitzchaki [Rashi], *Commentary on the Tanakh*, "Genesis 1:7," Sefaria.org, n.p., https://www.sefaria.org/Rashion_Genesis.1.7.2?lang=bi/ (1 October 2021).

nugget? We are not moving until you explain 'value judgment' and the term '*ki tov*.'" I will comply! **God could only render a judgment that something was good after the item was completely finished or formed.**

כִּי־טוֹב (*ki tov*, "that *it was* good") = "a judgment"

The separation of the lower waters **into Seas was incomplete on the second day**. On the third day, **two actions were completed**, so God discerned "כִּי־טוֹב" **twice**! One action concerned the completion of the waters, a process *Elohim started* on the second day. The second action concerned the vegetation, which *Elohim started and completed* on the same day—the third day. Do you see? Completion is the key. **An activity or entity must be completely finished before God could render judgment.**

Moreover, do you also recognize that judgment is not exclusively a negative concept? *Elohim* enacted "judgments" whenever He discerned "that *it was* good." The flip side is also true. On the second day, when God **did not discern**, "that *it was* good" He also made a judgment. Miners, we just excavated a dual-sided nugget. **God's actions and discernments in Genesis chapter 1 testify that *Elohim* operates exclusively by the Attribute of Strict Justice (Strict Judgments).**

At this point, perhaps you are wondering if **Adam** was cognizant of *Elohim*'s Attribute of Strict Justice. The answer is a formidable "yes" because Adam understood the concept of "value judgment days." *Adom* was created in Genesis 1:26, and Genesis 1:31 reads, "And *Elohim* discerned all that He made and behold (טוֹב מְאֹד, *tov me'ode*, excellent). And there were the evening and the morning sixth day" (Author's translation).[3] Hence**, everything else** God created on each of the previous days "was good." Although *Adom* was not *individually* rendered "excellent" on the sixth day, *Adom* can be included in "all that He made." Consequently, Adam had a definite frame of reference for God as *Elohim.*[4]

In Genesis 1 through Genesis 2:1–3, *Elohim* (אֱלֹהִים) occurred thirty-five times. However, from Genesis 2:4 until the end of chapter 4, the name *Elohim* is adjoined to a second name for God–"יְהוָה" (*Yehovah*), also known as The Tetragrammaton.[5] The result is "יְהוָה אֱלֹהִים" (The

---

[3]"*Adom*" is the transcription for the Hebrew word "אָדָם." When God creates humanity in Genesis 1:26–27, He uses two terms, *Adom* (אָדָם) and *Ha'Adom* (הָאָדָם). Both terms encompass the maleness (*za'char*) and the femaleness (*n'kay'vah*) that were abutted together (adjacent) in the first human being. In Genesis 1:26, אָדָם means **the first human being.** Many Bible translations render נַעֲשֶׂה אָדָם (*na'a'seh* ***Adom***) as "'Let us make man'" or "'Let us make mankind.'" My translation is "And *Elohim* said, 'Let us make ***Adom***'" (Author's translation). You may be surprised that the name "Adam," found in most English Bibles, is usually (**not always**) הָאָדָם (*Ha'Adom*) in Hebrew! The context frequently determines the correct meaning of אָדָם (*Adom*) and הָאָדָם (*Ha'Adom*) in the Hebrew Scriptures. For complex passages, what do we do?–excavate and mine. I told you Hebrew words have multiple nuances! Please see Appendix A-2.

[4]An astute person will ask, "Why does *Shabbat* not receive a '*ki tov*?'" The answer is too complex for this edition of *Your Sabbath Invitation.*

[5]The Tetragrammaton is a Greek term from the fifteenth century CE that means "four of something written" or "four letters." The four letters in יְהוָה are called The Tetragrammaton. In English, the most recognized Tetragrammaton for יְהוָה is "YHWH," usually pronounced "*Yahweh*" or "*Yehovah.*" I **only** mentioned "*Yehovah*" to help you grasp the concepts in this chapter. As your tour guide, I suggest that you finish reading chapter 10, then study Appendix A-3.

Eternal-*Elohim*). "The Eternal" in parentheses is a substitution for יְהוָה but not a transcription. Jews use alternative titles to avoid pronouncing the name יהוה and to ensure that no one ever violates "taking the name of The Eternal in vain" (Exodus 20:7, Author's translation) or fails to adhere to "You should be in awe of The Eternal" (Deuteronomy 6:13, Author's translation). In *Your Sabbath Invitation*, I primarily use the title "The Eternal." Table 12 shows the relationship between the names of God and the attributes of God in Genesis 1–4.

Table 12. The Names *Elohim* and The Eternal-*Elohim*

Verses	Names and Attributes
Genesis 1:1–2:3	אֱלֹהִים *Elohim* **Strict Justice**
Genesis 2:4–4:26 (end of chapter)	יְהוָה אֱלֹהִים The Eternal-*Elohim* **Mercy and Strict Justice**

After reviewing the table, you may wonder, "Why was יְהוָה added to *Elohim*?" My unusual response is: to temper *Elohim*'s justice. **The Hebrew names of God are not thoughtless or arbitrary; they are intentional, descriptive, and prophetic.** These statements might sound poetic, but what does "to temper *Elohim*'s justice" mean?

> *The Hebrew names of God are intentional and represent the attributes of God.*

In Genesis chapter 2, the **perfect Genesis 1** world is slightly transformed because a major change occurred. God's system of Strict Justice is intentionally disrupted by the advent of free will. Humanity is **the only creation God authorizes to function with free will**. In Genesis chapter 1, ***Adom* only knew God as *Elohim*–by His Attribute of Strict Justice**. When the concept of free will emerges in Genesis 2, perfect order disappears. As a result, God can no longer operate by Strict Justice alone. Now, He must temper Strict Justice with Mercy.[6] Without Mercy, human beings could face automatic destruction each time their free will violates God's perfect order.[7] **"The Eternal (יְהוָה, The Tetragrammaton)" represents God's Attribute of Mercy.**

> *Elohim* is God's Attribute of Strict Justice!

> God's Attribute of Mercy is The Tetragrammaton.

Attentive readers, are you puzzled or shocked? I hope so, and I know why. (One of my desires is to challenge your

---

[6]My statement is based on two *Aggadic midrashim* from *Pesikta Rabbati* and *Genesis Rabbah.* The first *midrash* states, "Initially, God intended to create it with the Attribute of Justice. But then He saw that the world cannot exist [with only Justice], so He gave priority to the Attribute of Mercy, and joined it with the Attribute of Justice" (Pesikta Rabbati 40). The second *midrash* says, "Thus said the Holy One, blessed be His name! 'If I create the world with the Attribute of Mercy, sin will abound; and if I create it with the Attribute of Justice, how can the world exist? Therefore I create it with both attributes, Mercy and Justice, and may it thus endure'" (Genesis Rabbah 12:15).

[7]Adam experienced *part* of God's mercy when God created the woman in Genesis 2. Through His matchless discernment, God proactively judged that Adam was alone and afterwards created אִשָּׁה (*isha*, woman). **Adam did not experience the epiphany of God's mercy as יְהוָה until Genesis 3 when the sin occurred.**

familiar conclusions about the Hebrew text.) Nowhere in the Scriptures is free will *stated explicitly* by the expression, "You shall have free will." So, when did free will enter and *explicitly* disrupt God's harmonious world? Students, free will is *implicitly* understood in Genesis 2:15–17:

- **Genesis 2:15** (Author's translation)
  "And **The Eternal-*Elohim*** (**יְהוָה אֱלֹהִים**) took *Ha'Adom* and placed him into the Garden of Eden **to work it and to guard it** (**לְעָבְדָהּ וּלְשָׁמְרָהּ**, ***l'av'dah oo'l'sham'rah***)."
- **Genesis 2:16** (Author's translation)
  "And **The Eternal-*Elohim*** (**יְהוָה אֱלֹהִים**) commanded *Ha'Adom* saying, 'from every tree of the Garden **you may surely eat** (**אָכֹל תֹּאכֵל**, ***a'chol toe'chel***).'"
- **Genesis 2:17** (Author's translation)
  "'And from [the] Tree of Knowledge of Good and Evil do not eat from it, **for on the day you eat from it, you will surely die** (**כִּי בְּיוֹם אֲכָלְךָ מִמֶּנּוּ מוֹת תָּמוּת**, ***ki b'yom a'chal'cha mi'meh'nu mot ta'mut***)."

Although God issued a mandate that included consequences for death, *Adom* still possessed a free will. This is no different than the death warnings written on every pack of cigarettes. Furthermore, the free will provision is required. Without the freedom to choose, **human beings would become mere robots, who live solely to fulfill what God desires (and commands), or face instant death.**

As your *moreh* (teacher), let me ask you another question regarding Adam. Could Adam have understood the idea of יְהוָה conceptually in Genesis 1 through Genesis 2:1–3, even though The Tetragrammaton was not yet introduced? My response is "Yes." Adam was intellectually capable, but no genuine precedent for יְהוָה existed before God authorized free will, during a situation of dire circumstances when one's life was on the line. While there are definite precedents for *Elohim* in Genesis 1–God discerned, "that *it was* good," and God also did not discern, "that *it was* good" on the second day–**there is no frame of reference for a dire situation in Genesis 1**. Genesis 1 consists of perfect order and precise value judgements.

From Genesis 2:4 and to the end of chapter 4, God's Attributes of Strict Justice and Mercy function conjointly. **God constantly balances justice and mercy, while simultaneously operating within the context of deferred punishments and human freedom**. As a result, some individuals may be more susceptible to disregarding or denying responsibility for their unlawful actions. Others may live wickedly and nonchalantly justify their behavior by claiming that there is no God. Their claim is based on a faulty conclusion that immediate justice is nonexistent. This is exactly the point of Psalm 92. Psalm 92 is Adam's confession that God's Strict Justice and Mercy **do co-exist**.

> *Only God can perfectly balance justice and mercy.*

On the Sabbath, Adam fully experienced and comprehended God's mercy because he did not die

instantly. During his epiphany, Adam also realized that a delay in strict justice could provoke an erroneous conclusion that the wicked always prosper. For this reason, Adam declares "It is good to praise The Eternal…" (Psalm 92:1, Author's translation). Adam fully recognized that every breath humanity will inhale is evidence of God's Attribute of Mercy (יְהוָה).

To continue, Adam was also cognizant that his progeny might mistake *Elohim*'s profound Mercy as a delay in justice, then falsely assume that God had abandoned the world and no longer cared. Therefore, Adam writes, "How profound are Your plans! The brutish man cannot know it, the fool cannot understand it. Though the wicked flourish like grass, and all evildoers thrive, it is only that they may be destroyed forever" (Psalm 92:6–8, Author's translation).

Adam was the first human being to warrant God's judgment, but he was also the first individual to experience God's Mercy. **When God rescued Adam, He also rescued all of humanity.** Adam's homage to the *Shabbat*, "*l'yom HaShabbat*," is not surprising because the Sabbath became a definite protection for Adam. God's judgment could not be executed on a day that He, God, had made holy (Genesis 2:3). So, **instead of receiving an immediate physical death, Adam received an opportunity to reflect on God's Mercy and to ask for forgiveness**. The overwhelming emotions (*mizmor shir*) associated with a new beginning prompted Adam to compose Psalm 92.

When God rescued Adam, He also rescued all of humanity!

You are alive today because of the original merciful act God bestowed on humanity. Therefore, please do not view the Sabbath invitation as an offer to a weekend barbecue! **God's Sabbath invitation is literally a pipeline to your ancestor Adam, who was freed from temporary life support in order to continue an intimate life with God.**

Notes

PART THREE

A day to give hearts to God

Chapter 11 Highlights

- Psalm 30 is the only other psalm that opens with a *mizmor shir*. Like Psalm 92, Psalm 30 was authored by Adam.
- Psalm 92 was "downloaded" and composed simultaneously. Psalm 30 contains a variety of themes. It was composed later, after its initial reception.
- Adam did not publicly confess his sin. Psalm 30 is Adam's repentance monologue to God based on an internal epiphany.
- Psalm 30 pays tribute to the inauguration of David's family. A *midrash* on Genesis 5:5 says that Adam gave seventy of his years to David. This allowed David to publicly confess his sins, exhibit genuine repentance, and live to sing praises to God.
- The Messiah comes through David's lineage. Adam's gift to David resulted in humanity's restoration through Messiah. אדם (*Adom*) is an acronym for Adam, David, and Messiah.

Your Sabbath Invitation

The Adam-David Connection

Salutations! How are you doing? Are you still enjoying the journey? To date, you have explored many sites, and most of them contained *midrashim.* The leading site was a *midrash* on Psalm 92, which grappled with Adam as the Psalm's author. As we approach the halfway point, you are already *dra'shing* like an expert! Well done! Before our next stop, relax as I summarize the *midrash* on Psalm 92.

Adam sinned on a Friday and expected immediate death as a punishment. To the contrary, he received God's unexpected, infinite mercy. On *Shabbat*, the day after the sin, Adam composed Psalm 92 and dedicated it "to the Sabbath Day" (*l'yom HaShabbat*), hinting that he experienced God's mercy on that sacred day. We discovered that the catalyst behind Psalm 92 is the rare *mizmor shir* at the beginning of verse 1 (the superscription). The *mizmor shir* confirms that Adam did not merely compose Psalm 92–he passionately and instantaneously downloaded its melody and lyrics. What a phenomenal tribute to the Sabbath! All right, grab your binoculars and Bibles for our survey of Psalm 30, the only other psalm that opens with a *mizmor shir*. We will also examine a *midrash* related to Genesis 5:5. Our examination will uncover some astounding nuggets and introduce you to the vital connection between Adam and David.

The *mizmor shir* is a fusion of two terms, *mizmor* and *shir*. The phrase **only** appears **at the beginning of two psalms: Psalm 92 and Psalm 30. Based on the rare appearances, I assert that Adam authored both Psalms,** but the composition histories of the two Psalms differ. In Psalm 92, Adam received ("downloaded") the lyrics and the melody together, then simultaneously composed the Psalm into its final form (see chapter 7). Psalm 30 follows the same downloading process, but **the Psalm's final form suggests that Adam composed Psalm 30 later–apart from his initial reception (download).**

The rare phrase mizmor shir only appears at the beginning of Psalm 92 and Psalm 30.

Previously, I described Psalm 92 as a song that "articulates praise and worship to God, accounts the downfall of the wicked, and highlights the flourishing of the righteous." The topical flow and structure of Psalm 92 are straightforward. In contrast, the topics in Psalm 30 swing like a pendulum–ranging from death to life–especially in verses, 4, 6, and 12. Table 13 shows the verses according to their numbering in the Hebrew Bible (verses 3, 5, and 11 in standard English translations).

Table 13. Sample Topics Found in Psalm 30

Psalm 30 from the Hebrew Bible (Author's translations)	
Verse 4	The Eternal, You brought up my soul from *Sheol*, You saved my life from going down to the pit.
Verse 6	For His anger lasts for a moment, His favor for a lifetime; weeping lingers at night, but joy [comes] in the morning.
Verse 12	You turned my mourning into dancing; You opened my sackcloth, and girded me with happiness…

Table 13 reveals a gamut of emotions and subjects. Adam nears death in verse 4 but enjoys dancing in verse 12. Verse 6 contrasts God's anger with His favor. In addition to the alternating sentiments and themes, Psalm 30 includes an amazing structural feature which Psalm 92 lacks. The structural difference consists of three verses, which uphold my observation and theory regarding a later and separate composition for Psalm 30. **The three verses comprise Adam's repentance monologue to God**.

Dear readers, I am detecting multiple questions from you, but three are obvious: "1) David, what is a '**repentance monologue to God**'?; 2) Why do you say Psalm 30 contains 'Adam's repentance monologue' when Scripture does not affirm that Adam repented?; and 3) Why do you ascribe authorship to Adam when the opening of Psalm 30 contains David's name?" First, the term "repentance monologue" is original and arises from my own personal analysis and ***dra'shing*** of Psalm 30. Second, the repentance monologue conveys Adam's **internal realization** concerning the magnitude of his sin. I contend that Adam fully recognized his Eden transgression *internally*, but he lacked the courage to *verbalize* his guilt to God *publicly*. The repentance monologue motif complements the *mizmor shir* in the beginning of Psalm 30 because a *mizmor shir* indicates "an instantaneous transfer of emotion and intellect, which manifests as a song following a traumatic life event." (See chapter 9, "Adam's Defense Attorney.") So, **Psalm 30 is not Adam's public confession. The monologue is Adam's internal epiphany and grateful recognition to God** for the new lease on life God bestowed on him.[1] The heart of the repentance monologue occurs in verses 9–11 as shown in Table 14 (next page).

Your third question is perceptive and correct. Nevertheless, mentioning David's name in the beginning does not prove he authored the Psalm! The superscription of Psalm 30 says, "A Psalm *and* Song *at* the dedication of the house of David" (KJV). As we learned in chapter 6,

---

[1]Adam's epiphany is that God is merciful, and *Shabbat* facilitated the epiphany. How? *Shabbat* prevented God from exercising judgment on Adam concerning his sin in the Garden of Eden. God could not execute Adam on *Shabbat*, a day that He had formerly sanctified as holy. In the midst of experiencing the goodness and infinite mercy of God, Adam begins to process his internal realization–"How did I get into this situation? I should be dead because my sin was deliberate and unjustified. Why am I still alive?"

Table 14. The Repentance Monologue in Psalm 30

Psalm 30 from the Hebrew Bible (Author's translations)	
Verse 9	To You, The Eternal, I called; to the Master I pleaded.
Verse 10	What profit is there in my blood in going down into the pit? Can dust acknowledge You? Can it proclaim Your truth?
Verse 11	Listen, The Eternal, and be gracious to me; The Eternal, be my helper.

superscriptions (titles) are Scripture in the Hebrew Bible. **Thus and hereafter, I will only use the Hebrew Bible's convention, which renders superscriptions as verses.**

Hereafter, to conform with the Hebrew Bible, superscriptions (titles) will be numbered as verses!

To continue, if you allow me to translate Psalm 30:1 verbatim, as "*Mizmor Shir* **to the inauguration** of the House of David,"[2] you will comprehend the true meaning of the verse. **The author is not paying tribute to a physical**

[2]I am fully aware that many versions translate Psalm 30:1 as "A Psalm. A song for the dedication of the temple. Of David" (NIV®). The problem with this approach is that the Psalm in no way concerns Temple rituals or sacrifices. Strictly speaking, Psalm 30 is a thanksgiving psalm from a single individual, namely, Adam.

building, more accurately, he is acknowledging the beginnings, that is "inauguration," of a family. As you finish the Psalm, you will realize that the songwriter endured a traumatic emotional ordeal, in effect, a near-death experience. The Psalm says, "The Eternal (The Tetragrammaton), You have brought my soul from *Sheol*; You have resuscitated me from my descent into the pit" (Author's translation, Psalm 30:4 in the Hebrew Bible; v. 3 in most English Bibles). The songwriter elaborates further, "What profit is there in my blood by my going down to the grave? Can dust praise You–proclaim Your truthfulness?" (Author's translation, Psalm 30:10 in the Hebrew Bible and v. 9 in many English translations). What is transpiring in this psalm?

In Psalm 30:1, the author is acknowledging the inauguration of a family.

Firstly, the person uttering these words is requesting a supernatural deliverance from death. By now, you understand that the *mizmor shir* in Psalm 30:1 signifies that intense emotions are connected to the author. **Therefore–coupled with our understanding that Adam authored Psalm 92–we may conclude Adam also composed Psalm 30.** With that being said, may I ask, if trauma and deliverance are the primary themes in Psalm 30, why does Adam begin the Psalm by paying homage to the initiation of David's family?

Adam authored Psalm 92 and he also composed Psalm 30.

There is a *midrash* stating that God showed Adam all his future generations. Almost immediately, Adam saw that David would die a few hours after his birth. Grieved by this prospective loss, Adam sought God, discovered that he himself had 1,000 years to live, then promptly offered to give seventy of his years to David. God accepted Adam's gift. **The *midrash* establishes an Adam-David connection** and is based on a potentially redundant phrase in Genesis 5:5, "And all the days of Adam, that he lived, were nine hundred and thirty years; and he died" (Author's translation).[3] The "redundancy" is "that he lived" (אֲשֶׁר־חַי, *asher chai*).

> *A midrash teaches that Adam offered seventy of his 1000 years to David.*

In my opinion, the verse could have excluded "*asher chai*" and read, "And all the days of Adam were nine hundred and thirty years." In fact, **none of the verses in Genesis 5 that recount the life span of Adam's descendants contain the phrase "that he lived" (*asher chai*).** However, God authored the Torah, not me! Therefore, Jewish hermeneutics compels me to ask the more astute questions: why does Genesis 5:5 include the words "that he lived" and what does "that he lived" really mean?

One possible answer for both questions is **"that he lived" can be interpreted as "that he (only) lived" or "that he (in actuality) lived,"** implying that Adam was supposed to

---

[3]The *Midrash* is called the *Yalkut Shimoni*. See *Yalkut Shimoni* on Torah 41, https://www.sefaria.org/Yalkut_Shimoni_on_Torah.41?lang=bi/ (20 April 2021).

live longer. From the perspective of the *midrash*, Adam decided to give seventy years from his own life, in order to extend David's life, enabling David to reign as king and sing praises to God.

A fascinating inference from the *midrash* is that Adam must have observed multiple facets of David's *extended* life, including his sin with Bathsheba and his other infractions. **Despite David's failings, Adam was still willing to give his remaining seventy years on earth to King David.**

David was not a perfect human being. When Nathan the Prophet confronted David for his sin with Bathsheba, David said, "I have sinned against The Eternal" (2 Samuel 12:13, Author's translation). In Psalm 51, David beseeched God, "blot out my transgressions" and "Return to me the joy of your salvation" (Author's translation). God forgave David, removed his sins, and David did not die. On the contrary, when Adam sinned, he hid, and God asked him, "Where are you?" (Genesis 3:9). **In that moment, Adam could have repented immediately and requested forgiveness from God, but he chose another path.**[4] As an alternative and without hesitation, he passed the guilt to another human being–the only other human being in existence–his wife Eve (*Chavah*).

The combined consequences of willful disobedience, of eating from [the] Tree of the Knowledge of Good and

---

[4]Although Adam received and experienced the Psalm 30 repentance monologue within himself, he *still* missed the opportunity to repent. In modern vernacular, "God put Adam's back against the wall." Unfortunately, Adam lacked David's boldness, courage, and humility. Adam never declared, "חָטָאתִי" (*cha'ta'ti*, I sinned).

I mentioned earlier that the structure and content of Psalm 30

Evil, and of not seizing the decisive moment of repentance continue to affect all of humanity today. In contrast, **David's willful sins, coupled with his genuine repentance, opened the door for a complete restoration of his relationship with God!**

Adam had a positive incentive for giving seventy years of his life: **He would grant David the opportunity to succeed where he himself had failed.** This point is significant and is related to the repentance monologue. Grab your pickaxes right now! You will need them for the advanced mining ahead.

Repentance was —and still is— a gift from God!

Contextually, the repentance monologue highlights Adam, but linguistically it involves **three biblical persons** and the Hebrew word "חָטָאתִי" (*cha'ta'ti*, I sinned). **The first person is Adam**, who is the first human being to *internalize* that he sinned, but he did not *publicly* or *verbally* admit his guilt to God. Psalm 30 does not contain the word

---

opposes **a simultaneous download and composing** of the Psalm as we witnessed with Psalm 92. Frankly, there are many undisclosed intricacies in Psalm 30 that apply to *Shabbat* and to the events in Genesis 3:6–9, but they exceed discussion in *Your Sabbath Invitation.* In fact, the intricacies astounded then compelled me to pause and reflect further. Yet, one point I can confidently disclose is that **the repentance monologue in Psalm 30 was simultaneously downloaded and composed on *Shabbat*, before Adam was expelled from the Garden of Eden**. Does this suggest that the remaining verses in Psalm 30 (verses 1–8 and 12–13) were downloaded and composed **in unison after** *Shabbat* or outside the Garden of Eden? Perhaps! In the future, if God permits, I or someone else may mine and decipher verses 1–8 and 12–13.

חָטָאתִי. **The second figure is Judah** and concerns his incident with Tamar in Genesis 38:26. Judah admitted his guilt in the court of his day, but he too never expressed the wrong *verbally* with the word חָטָאתִי (*cha'ta'ti*, I sinned). Finally, in 2 Samuel 12:13, **David not only *internalized* that he had sinned, but he is the first person to express his wrongdoing *verbally* and *publicly* with the word חָטָאתִי (*cha'ta'ti*)** and the **first to authenticate his confession with genuine repentance.**[5]

> *David is the first to authentically confess "חָטָאתִי" (cha'ta'ti, I sinned).*

Therefore, what Adam sees in David when he gives him seventy years of his life is the repentance that he failed to do or to declare in the Garden of Eden. (Adam never said *cha'ta'ti* and David did!) What Adam lost in the Garden of Eden would be reclaimed through the House of David. Adam's gift to David secured David's lineage.

At this point, I would like to mine one additional nugget related to the Adam-David connection. According to another

---

[5]During the locust plague, Pharaoh admitted *publicly* to Moses and to Aaron that he sinned against God (Exodus 10:16). He also used the term *cha'ta'ti* twice (vv. 16–17). However, after the locust plague, Pharaoh clearly demonstrated no true remorse. Pharaoh sought to placate God temporarily to avoid dying from the devastation of the plague. In contrast, David repented immediately after his sin and even composed Psalm 51 to urge God to restore completely the relationship He and David previously shared. David's sincere repentance proves why God documented him as the one "who kept my commands and followed me with all his heart" (1 Kings 14:8). Acts 13:22 says that David was "a man after My [God's] heart" (Author's translation).

midrash, which we cannot explore here, the Hebrew name for Adam contains the nugget. Adam's name אדם (*Adom*) consists of three Hebrew letters: aleph ("א"), dalet ("ד"), and mem ("ם"). **The name אדם (*Adom*) is an acronym representing the initials of three people–Adam (אדם), David (דוד), and Messiah (משיח, *Mashiach*)–there's the nugget!** Table 15 depicts this amazing gem.

Table 15. The אָדָם (*Adom*) Acronym (read right to left)

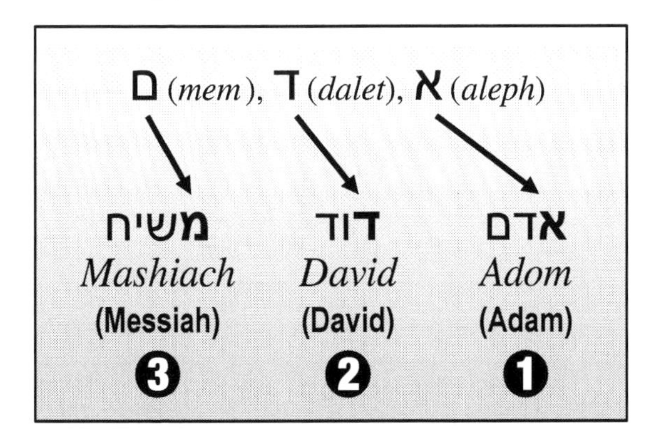

In Table 15 you will see 1, 2, and 3. From top to bottom, number 1 identifies the Hebrew word אדם, then the transliteration *Adom*, and finally, the English translation Adam. Right now, apply the same technique to number 2 and to number 3. Did you uncover the gem?

So far, I have only discussed Adam and David, the first two names from the אדם (*Adom*) acronym, because I wanted you to appreciate the magnitude of the Adam-David connection as revealed in Psalm 30:1 and as explained by the *midrash* for Genesis 5:5. **Incredible! Through our gem, the acronym, we have discovered that Messiah is**

joined to Adam and David because Messiah arises from David's house.

By giving seventy years to David, Adam initiates the restoration of humanity. Messiah arises from David's house, and eventually all people will acknowledge God.[6]

---

[6]See Isaiah 45:23.

Notes

PART FOUR

A day of partnership and purpose

Chapter 12 Highlights

- *Shabbat* encompasses a Divine partnership between you and God—to proclaim His existence and to actualize His plan for a relationship with humanity.
- *Shabbat* is the culmination and masterpiece of God's creation.
- The Ten Commandments (Ten Categorical Statements) *explicitly* mandate the Sabbath. However, Genesis 2:1–3 contains an *implicit* expectation for humanity to observe *Shabbat*.
- The Hebrew Torah Scroll is divided into units of text called *parshiyot* (singular, *parsha*), not chapters and verses.
- Each day of creation has its own *parsha*. The *parsha* for the seventh day is Genesis 2:1–3.
- Mining verbal redundancies in the seventh day *parsha* will help answer the question: Did God complete His creation on the sixth day or on the seventh?
- The Sabbath is a life-giving necessity, just like oxygen!

Your Sabbath Invitation

Redundancies and Parshiyot

Until now, I have presented *Shabbat* as an invitation–an opportunity to participate in the Isaiah 66:23 Messianic prophecy. By now you know new facts about the Sabbath that you did not know before. For instance, *Shabbat* is a pipeline to access God's original merciful act toward humanity. You also know that **the Sabbath is God's Divine request to spend T-I-M-E with you!** Through His Sabbath invitation, the Creator of the Universe conveys His love for you.

Although the Sabbath invitation exceeds any human entreaty, you may still have ongoing reservations about accepting the heavenly request. Yet, in your delay, please stay alert! I hope you will not mark the invitation as "Important, consider later" or store it nonchalantly on your desk where it could be ignored. In this chapter we will investigate another aspect about *Shabbat* which may render God's invitation more appealing and essential.

I have already suggested obstacles that could hinder Christians from participating in *Shabbat*. The first possible hindrance was time: "The Sabbath may disrupt your present routine and schedule." Perhaps your weekends are too busy to consider a *Shabbat* celebration; Friday night through Sunday evening is your time to unwind from a hectic work week. You might reserve the weekly two-day hiatus for achieving personal, family, and career goals. To stop and drop your entire world every Friday night at sundown is probably impossible to imagine or accomplish; and I certainly hear your comments, "David, from the standpoint of time–there is no time!"

From another perspective, is it possible that *Shabbat* has a greater purpose than adding another task to your schedule? For example, *Shabbat* encompasses a Divine partnership between you and God! **God desires for you to proclaim His existence and actualize His plan to have a flourishing relationship with humanity.**

With this in mind, would you now be willing to reclassify and upgrade His Sabbath invitation from "Important" to "Urgent"? To help your decision, I will mine some biblical "redundancies" to show you the grandeur of *Shabbat*. As God created the stars, plants, wildlife, and humanity, He also created *Shabbat*. ***Shabbat* is the culmination and masterpiece of God's creation!**

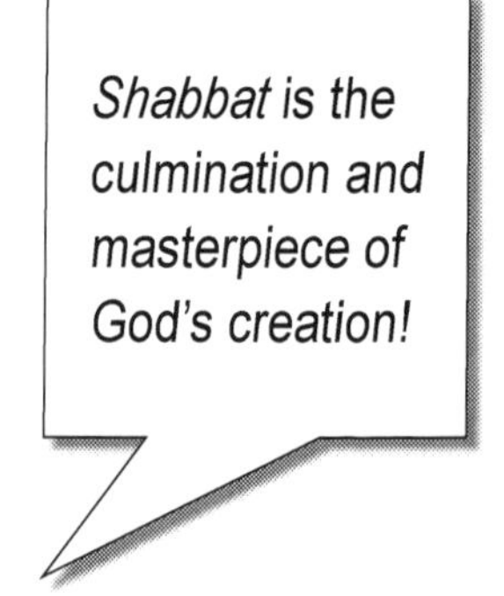

Most of you know that God **explicitly** mandated the Sabbath in Exodus 20 and Deuteronomy 5, the Ten Commandments (Ten Categorical Statements). Did you also know that Genesis 2:1–3 contain an **implicit expectation** for humanity to observe *Shabbat*? To prove my statement, we will mine Genesis 2:1–3 for revelation–but not quickly. That text is a principal site, and the mining requires detailed information and two steps. **Step one** concerns *two Hebrew treasures*. **Step two** involves a *mountaintop revelational nugget*, which we will discover in the next chapter. Therefore, sit back, clean your trowels and buckets, think Hebraically, and take some exceptional notes. To **effectively mine the** Genesis 2:1–3 site, **we must read the passages in a Hebrew Torah Scroll**–the *first Hebrew treasure*.[1]

THE TORAH SCROLL:
Congregational Readings of Torah

How many of you have observed the public reading of Scriptures during a synagogue service? Did the speaker or reader use the same Bible devices millions use each week when listening to sermons in their churches? Today, millions of pastors and church members read the Scriptures from smartphones, Bible apps, tablets, or laptops.[2] Others follow the sermon using traditional book forms of the Bible. Frequently, and for various reasons, many churches also project the Bible verses on a screen.

---

[1]Consult the Glossary for a definition of a "Torah Scroll."

[2]My use of "pastors" does not exclude other leaders who preach or teach in congregations such as, ministers, elders, reverends, bishops, priests, deacons, and others.

Not only do the resources vary, but so do the Bible translations. Some ministers teach exclusively from one version, while others employ several. Regardless of the version or translation, all of today's Bibles possess a common trait: they identify Scriptures by numbered chapters and verses. Archbishop Stephen Langton originally developed chapters for the Christian Bibles (Old and New Testaments) in the thirteenth century CE. In 1555, Robert Estienne, also called Stephanus, formulated the verse numbers for the New Testament, and they are still applicable today.[3] Although chapters and verse numbers are uniform, no universal Christian law or practice requires Bibles to be formatted and printed according to one particular standard. This is not true in Judaism. **The entire layout of the Scriptures on scrolls is standardized.**

In Jewish law and practice, certain **mandated Scriptures from the Pentateuch** are read publicly to the congregation on Mondays, Thursdays, Sabbaths, and on Jewish holidays–with a quorum of at least ten people present. **Such texts must be read from a Torah Scroll.** The Torah Scroll is *the first of the two treasures* I mentioned earlier. A Torah Scroll comprises the Pentateuch, namely the **five Books of Moses–Genesis, Exodus, Leviticus, Numbers, and Deuteronomy**.

A Torah Scroll contains the Pentateuch.

[3]I have only provided basic information on the chapter and verse divisions in the Hebrew Bible and the New Testament. The full history is complex. For elucidation concerning the Hebrew Bible, I recommend Jordan S. Penkower, "Verse Divisions in the Hebrew Bible," *Vetus Testamentum*, vol. 50, fasc. 3 (July, 2000): 379–393, https://www.jstor.org/stable/1585296/ (15 December 2021).

Orthodox Jews never read Scriptures specifically **mandated for the congregation** using printed versions or digital formats of the Bible. **While there are mandates that govern the readings from a Torah Scroll, strict mandates also exist for scripting a Torah Scroll.** First and foremost, according to Deuteronomy 31:19 and 22, scripting a Torah Scroll is a supreme, religious endeavor. Therefore, the sacred Scroll must be handwritten by a pious scribe (*sofer*) using a quill and a special ink.[4] The Torah is written on sheets of parchment from a kosher animal. Eventually, skilled *soferim* (plural of *sofer*) sew the parchment sheets together using kosher sinews called *gidim.*[5] Each sheet contains the biblical text, arranged in a prescribed number of columns–ranging from three to eight columns. Each column of text may contain forty-two to sixty lines. The length of each line equals the horizontal length of thirty letters. Torah Scrolls require approximately a year to complete.[6]

In Jewish law, the Torah Scroll is the Incarnate Embodiment of God's will, so we regard the Scroll with extreme sanctity. In fact, synagogue members will donate monies or provide the components to accessorize a Torah Scroll, which may include a crown and assorted vestments.

---

[4]A *sofer* is a specially trained individual who transcribes sacred Jewish texts from the Torah and from other religious works. The texts for a Torah scroll are copied onto kosher parchment using the traditional form of Hebrew calligraphy.

[5]The *gidim* are special threads made from the veins of a kosher animal. Kosher animals include deer, goats, bulls, and cows.

[6]The intricacies of preparing the parchment, ink, quill as well as the precise writing and spacing of the Hebrew letters and words exceed the scope of *Your Sabbath Invitation.*

If a Torah Scroll becomes invalid following certain types of damage such as, portions of the text being burned in a fire, **we are obligated to bury the Scroll**. Unusable Torah Scrolls are never discarded in the trash because the Scroll is a Divine composition.

Formatting the Torah Scroll

Unlike the bound versions of the Hebrew Bible, Hebrew Torah Scrolls do not contain chapters, verses, or punctuation marks, and the Hebrew letters in a Torah Scroll are written without the *nikudot*.[7] The *nikudot* are Hebrew vowels. To appreciate their importance, imagine your English Bibles written without the vowels a, e, i, o, u, and y. Would you read the Scriptures effortlessly or struggle to pronounce the words correctly? Similarly, the person who reads the **mandated Hebrew Scriptures** to the congregation must know **how to annunciate every word properly**, without the presence of the *nikudot*. What a task!

The formatting process for a Torah Scroll also includes ***parshiyot***, units of texts separated by an empty space. **There are two types of *parshiyot*, open and closed.** The tradition of the *parshiyot* precedes the formation of chapters and verses. The *parshiyot* represent the *second Hebrew treasure*.

On the next page, Figure 3 depicts a photograph of a column from an actual Torah Scroll. The column consists of forty-two lines. Within the column there are two closed

---

[7]The word *nikudot* is plural. The singular is *nikud*. Read a full explanation of "*nikud, nikudot*" in the Glossary.

parshiyot and one open *parsha* (singular for *parshiyot*). Can you find them without looking at the answer?

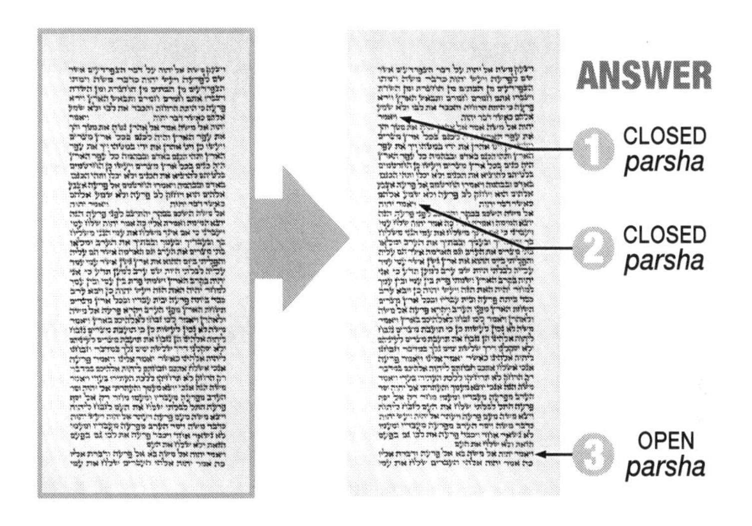

Figure 3. Open and Closed *Parshiyot* in a Torah Scroll

The spacing between the two units of text defines whether a *parsha* is open or closed. When you examine the figure, you will see a space between the first unit of text and the second unit of text, and **both units are on the same line. The second unit is defined as a closed *parsha* because it starts on the same line where the first unit ends.** Arrow 1 in Figure 3 indicates the beginning of the first **closed *parsha***. Remember, **a *parsha* is a portion of biblical text, not the empty space**. Please follow the same technique to locate the second closed *parsha* using arrow 2.

How are you doing? I hope you detected the closed *parshiyot* successfully because the form of the **open *parsha*** is entirely different. Look at arrow 3, and observe its position **on the next line**. Arrow 3 marks the beginning of the **open *parsha***. (In this example, the open *parsha* continues into the next Torah column which is not shown in Figure 3.) Here is a useful reminder: open *parshiyot* **always begin on the far right**, but closed *parshiyot* can begin **anywhere** on a line of text.

Friends and miners, this concludes **Step one** of our excavation. Excellent! We have just studied *the two Hebrew treasures*: **the Torah Scroll and the *parshiyot***. You are now well-equipped to distinguish open and closed *parshiyot*. You also comprehend that **Torah Scrolls are highly revered in Judaism and proper formatting of the biblical text is mandatory. The *parshiyot* have utmost importance in the formatting process.**

> *A **closed parsha** begins on the same line as the previous unit of text, separated by a designated space. An **open parsha** begins on a new line.*

Excavating the Parshiyot

Students, I hope you took excellent notes and are well prepared. Did you fully comprehend my description of the *parshiyot*? I hope so because I am ready to leave the bus. If you need more time to review the material, **I will wait for you**. To mine Genesis 2:1–3 properly, **you must understand the difference between closed and open *parshiyot***.

When you are ready to disembark, I have a wonderful announcement: the Genesis 2:1–3 passages in your Bible are actually **one *parsha*** in a Torah Scroll. Many of you just shouted, "Whoa David! How can all of those verses be contained in **one *parsha***?" To astound you further–**all the days of creation, including the seventh day, are individual *parshiyot***, that is, **separate units of text**. Look at the Torah Scroll in Figure 4 depicting the *parshiyot* for the seven days of creation. **Notice that all of them are open.**

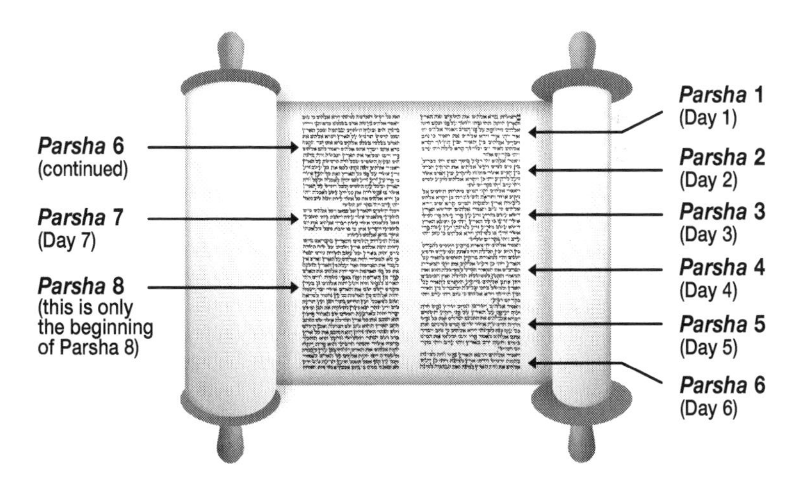

Figure 4. The Torah Scroll: Genesis columns 1 and 2

The notion that **each day of creation and the seventh day exist as a separate *parsha* should compel us to stop and profoundly reflect on these important biblical units**. Table 16 matches the first eight *parshiyot* to the modern references for Genesis 1:1 through 3:15 (see next page).

Table 16. The First Eight *Parshiyot* for Genesis 1:1–3:15

Torah Scroll *Parshiyot*	Creation Day	Verse References in Modern English Bibles
1st *parsha*	Day 1	Genesis 1:1–5
2nd *parsha*	Day 2	Genesis 1:6–8
3rd *parsha*	Day 3	Genesis 1:9–13
4th *parsha*	Day 4	Genesis 1:14–19
5th *parsha*	Day 5	Genesis 1:20–23
6th *parsha*	Day 6	Genesis 1:24–31
7th *parsha*	Day 7	Genesis 2:1–3
8th *parsha* *A lot of stories transpire in this section, including the creation of the first human being, the naming of the animals, the surgery to make Eve (Chavah), and more.*		Genesis 2:4–3:15

In Table 16 we see that Genesis 1:31 is the last line of the 6th *parsha*. The verse states "God saw all that He had made, and it was excellent. And there was evening, and there was morning–the sixth day" (Author's translation). In modern English translations, Genesis 1:31 is the last verse in Genesis chapter 1, but the *sofer* did not conclude the *parsha* at Genesis 1:31 for convenience, to preserve space, or to follow contemporary chapter and verse numbers! While I cannot elaborate further, as your guide I can assure you that **closed and open *parshiyot* are not accidental or meaningless**. Therefore, appreciating the structure of the *parshiyot*, especially the 6th *parsha*, will help us mine some exciting features in the Genesis 2:1–3 passages: the redundancies.

Redundancies

Friends, we just left the bus, and a *mountain of redundancies* is in view. Relax! The mountain is not Everest or Hermon. Remember, the main purpose of this chapter is to recognize that the Genesis 2:1–3 passages **contain an implicit mandate** for humanity to celebrate *Shabbat*. **That mandate** lies on the mountain's summit, and our only immediate task is to climb the mountain. In the next chapter, we will fully excavate (decode) Genesis 2:1–3 after we have reached the mountaintop. Right now, grab your spades and trowels because the path up the mountain is completely exegetical!

Let us begin with **Genesis 1:31**, which is the last line of the 6th *parsha*–"*Elohim* discerned all that he had made, and it was excellent. And there was evening, and there was morning–the sixth day" (Author's translation). The *parsha* emphasizes that God completed creation **on the sixth day.**

Now move to the 7th *parsha* of the Torah Scroll where Genesis 2:1–3 reside. Miners, get ready! We are going to explore my English translation of the Genesis passages by starting with three verbs found in Table 17.

Turn the page and locate the underlined words "completed," "did," and "ceased." In Genesis 2:1 we are told that the physical creation was completed. In Genesis 2:2, my Author's translation says, **"with the seventh day."** Most English Bibles state "on the seventh day," "by the

Table 17. Genesis 2:1–3: Verbs Underlined (Author's translation)

2:1	Now the heavens and the earth were <u>completed</u> and all their host.
2:2	And *Elohim* <u>completed</u> with the seventh day His work that He <u>did</u>, and He <u>ceased</u> with the seventh day from all His work that He <u>did</u>.
2:3	And *Elohim* blessed the seventh day, and He sanctified it when He <u>ceased</u> from all His work which *Elohim* had created to do.

seventh day," or a combination of both phrases. So, when we compare Genesis 1:31 and Genesis 2:2, a question arises: **Did God complete His creation on the sixth day or on the seventh?**[8]

Answering the question requires the **Jewish redundancy hermeneutic**, Tables 16 and 17, and your best mining skills. Revisit Table 17 for the *potentially* redundant verbs—completed, did, and ceased. If I were the Bible's editor, I would condense Genesis 2:1–3 (the 7th *parsha* in Table 16) into one line: "God ceased, blessed, and sanctified the seventh day." Then, I would insert my newly designed line **at the end of Genesis 1:31**, establishing it as the last line of the 6th *parsha*. As a result, Genesis 2:1–3 vanishes and

[8]The same question pertains to the preposition "by": **did God complete His creation by the sixth day or by the seventh?**

God's original 8th *parsha* in Table 16 becomes my 7th *parsha*. Snap! I boldly "call it a day" (pun intended) and entitle the rendition, the David Nekrutman Version (DNV)– a direct, uncomplicated work, free of *potential* redundancies. Table 18 unveils the DNV:

Table 18. The *David Nekrutman Version of the 7 Parshiyot*

1st *parsha*	**Day 1**	**Genesis 1:1–5**
2nd *parsha*	**Day 2**	**Genesis 1:6–8**
3rd *parsha*	**Day 3**	**Genesis 1:9–13**
4th *parsha*	**Day 4**	**Genesis 1:14–19**
5th *parsha*	**Day 5**	**Genesis 1:20–23**
NEW 6th *parsha*	**Days 6 and 7 (combined)**	**Genesis 1:24–NEW 1:31 (2:1–3 condensed and relocated to end of 1:31)**
NEW 7th *parsha* (previously the 8th *parsha*)		**Genesis 2:4–3:15**

In the first column of Table 18, Days 6 and 7 are now combined. The second column concerns the *parshiyot*. In the DNV translation, there are only seven *parshiyot* instead of eight. Finally, the third column introduces a new verse 31 (the Bible verse I changed) and deletes Genesis 2:1–3. Notice that **Genesis 2:4–3:15** remain unchanged. Miners, let me ask you, "In the end, is the DNV worth pursuing?" Absolutely not!

I assure you, the *David Nekrutman Version* (DNV) of Genesis is only imaginary. While my version eliminates *potential* redundancies, God is the Creator and Designer of Torah, not me!

Instead of rewording and removing perplexing areas of the text, I am compelled to mine revelation in order to resolve my earlier question: "**Did God complete His creation on the sixth day or on the seventh?** I will answer this question in the next chapter. **Hopefully, our brief excavation will inspire you to remove the Sabbath invitation from the *important events folder* and reclassify it in the *life-giving necessity file* because the Sabbath is just like oxygen.**

Notes

Chapter 13 Highlights

- There are several ways to translate Genesis 2:2 because the Hebrew preposition "בַּ" (*ba*) has several meanings.
- בַּ (*ba*) translated "with" conveys a meaning of "simultaneously." God was creating the world to the last millisecond before *Shabbat* began. He created His masterpiece, *Shabbat*, in the last millisecond!
- *B'rei'shit*, the first word in the Bible, can be mined to prove that God's last creative act was His original intention.
- The first three Hebrew words in the Bible are grammatically awkward, yet other possible expressions are unacceptable. Our conclusion is to never tamper with God's grammar!
- The שַׁבָּת (*Shabbat*) anagram hermeneutic proves that at the beginning, God wanted humanity to develop their awe of *Shabba*t.
- *Shabbat* becomes the platform for our actions during the week.

Your Sabbath Invitation

The Last Millisecond

Friends, we now have one question on the schedule–"Did God complete His creation on the sixth day or on the seventh day?" This apparently simple question is loaded with wide grammatical turns, famous detours, and deep rabbit holes. As your conscientious *moreh* (teacher), I strived to avoid these departures so that you could grasp two nuggets in Genesis 1:1. To discover the treasures, we must start in Genesis 2:1–3. Table 19 on page 134 presents Genesis 2 from a Hebraic perspective.

In the table, notice the following:

1. The name of God as "*Elohim*" appears three times.
2. The phrase "with the seventh day" (בַּיּוֹם הַשְּׁבִיעִי, *ba'yom ha'sh'vi'e*) is mentioned twice.

Table 19. Genesis 2:1–3 (Author's translation)

❶ And the heavens and the earth were completed and all their host.		
❷ And *Elohim* completed	with the seventh day בַּיּוֹם הַשְּׁבִיעִי (*ba'yom ha'sh'vi'e*)	His work that He did, (***a'sa***)
and He ceased	with the seventh day בַּיּוֹם הַשְּׁבִיעִי (*ba'yom ha'sh'vi'e*)	from all His work that He did. (***a'sa***)
❸ And *Elohim* blessed	the seventh day,	
and He sanctified	it	when
He ceased		from all His work which
Elohim had created (***bara***)		to do. (***la'a'sot***)

In many English Bible translations, Genesis 2:2 reads, "And on the seventh day God finished His work...," suggesting that God is *still* finishing His creation on the seventh day. To avoid the notion that God worked on *Shabbat*, several other translations render *ba'yom ha'sh'vi'e* as "by the seventh day," expecting the word "by" to provide sufficient ambiguity.[1] I chose another route and deliberately translated *ba'yom ha'sh'vi'e* "with the seventh day." Technically, there are several possible translations for בַּיּוֹם הַשְּׁבִיעִי (*ba'yom ha'sh'vi'e*) because the prefix preposition "בַּ" (*ba*) has several meanings:

1. "on"
2. "by"
3. "with"
4. "in"

Recall that in Jewish exegesis, every word of Scripture is significant–even the tiny preposition "בַּ" (*ba*). Thus, we interpret "בַּ" (*ba*) according to the context of the verse. In our *parsha* for Genesis 2, I recognized a distinct priority for the translation "with the seventh day" because the preposition "with" (*ba*) conveys "simultaneously." **When God was creating His masterpiece *Shabbat*, He was also creating the world to the last millisecond before *Shabbat* began**. According to Jewish tradition, God created several things at the twilight of the first Sabbath Eve including:

1. The rainbow that was designated as the sign of the Noahide covenant (Genesis 9:12–17)

---

[1]For numerous examples of "on the seventh day" and "by the seventh day," see *BibleGatewayOnline*, "Genesis 2:2," *BibleGateway.com*, n.p., https://www.biblegateway.com/verse/en/Genesis%202:2/ (29 September 2021).

2. The Manna that miraculously sustained the Israelites in the desert (Exodus 16:11–36)
3. The mouth of Miriam's well (Numbers 20:2; 21:36)
4. Moses' staff (Exodus 4:2–5)
5. The Tablets for the Ten Commandments (Ten Categorical Statements) (Exodus 32:15–16)[2]

God is entirely omnipotent. He can transition smoothly from the sixth day to the seventh while also creating multiple phenomena at twilight. **All of God's creative actions and His transition from work to a complete cessation occur *with the incoming* of the seventh day, not "on" or "by" the seventh day.** Hence, "with" is a more accurate interpretation for "בַ" (*ba*) in Genesis 2:2. So, the answer to the "simple" question, "Did God complete His creation on the sixth day or on the seventh day?" is, "neither." God did not complete creation **on** the sixth day or **on** the seventh. **God could have created the world in one millisecond, yet, He extended creation into six days, working to the last moment right before the seventh day.** God did not create the world in one millisecond, He **finished**

God finished creation in the last millisecond of the sixth day.

[2]See Mishnah Avot 5:6 for the entire list.

creation in one millisecond. Our bus tour is about to get interesting! The millisecond is the clue to the first nugget.

The phenomenon of the millisecond explains the culmination of creative activities and the transition from work to a full cessation, but the phenomenon itself is undetectable with our eyes or under a microscope. Nevertheless, what we can observe are the **outcomes** of the millisecond, which are ceasing, blessing, and sanctification. What do ceasing, blessing, and sanctification represent? They represent the Sabbath. **God created *Shabbat*–God's masterpiece–*with* the magnificent millisecond**. My dear readers, this is the first nugget: **God's last creative act was His original intention**. Take a moment to reflect on this profound statement. All the brushstrokes of the first six days were leading to God's *magnum opus–Shabbat*. God is The Artist who **intentionally** sketched each aspect of creation. Nothing in His creative process was haphazard.

The Magnificent Nugget, בְּרֵאשִׁית, and Shabbat

So far, the current journey has included: the last millisecond, the masterpiece, a *magnum opus*, and the magnificent nugget. We also resolved the opening question about *Shabbat* and the sixth or seventh days. Now we have room for another inquiry–one that concerns the **magnificent nugget** (God's last creative act was His original intention). Did God *always* intend for *Shabbat* to be the seventh day or for the seventh day to be *Shabbat*? Is the **magnificent nugget a true gem or a false statement?**

What do you think? To answer these questions, we must mine "בְּרֵאשִׁית" (***B'rei'shit***), the first word in the Hebrew Bible.

Many of you probably recognize ***B'rei'shit*** by sight or by sound. **The word *B'rei'shit*** is rare, but it still overflows with surprises. Most English Bibles usually translate ***B'rei'shit*** as "In the beginning." ***B'rei'shit*** only appears five times in the Hebrew Scriptures (Genesis 1:1; Jeremiah 26:1; 27:1; 28:1; 49:34), and **only** in Genesis 1:1 is ***B'rei'shit*** an unexpected, **awkward** term. To mine this revelational word, you will need to know two Jewish hermeneutical concepts:

> *Only in Genesis 1:1 is B'rei'shit an unexpected, awkward term.*

1. **Awkward Hebrew expressions and grammar are opportunities to decode more than what the finite text is presenting.**
2. There are Hebrew terms in the Bible, based on Jewish tradition, that are **anagrams**, where letters can be rearranged into other words, to provide deeper insights into the text.

The above hermeneutics may be new to you, but the idea that the Bible is also a code that connects to the infinite Heavenly Torah is already in your biblical interpretive arsenal. If you feel equipped, follow me.

Most English Bibles open Genesis 1:1 with, "In the beginning God created the heavens and the earth." The portion "In the beginning God created" sounds ***uncomplicated and grammatically correct* in English, but the parallel Hebrew text**, "בְּרֵאשִׁית בָּרָא אֱלֹהִים" (*B'rei'shit bara Elohim*) is ***complex and grammatically awkward***.[3] In addition, the English translation contains five words, but the Hebrew text encompasses three, "בְּרֵאשִׁית בָּרָא אֱלֹהִים" (*B'rei'shit bara Elohim*). Some of you are not moved by the inequality of the word count; others may be shocked. "David, I thought English Bible translations had a *one-to-one correspondence* with the Hebrew text." Dear students, let me prepare you for even greater wonders by singing, "We've Only Just Begun"![4] Therefore, buckle your seatbelts and shine your binoculars. Find your cell phones, notebooks, or Bibles and turn to Genesis 1:1. Our *beginning* starts with the Hebrew grammar of בְּרֵאשִׁית בָּרָא אֱלֹהִים (*B'rei'shit bara Elohim*).

Unpacking Genesis 1:1

To unpack בְּרֵאשִׁית בָּרָא אֱלֹהִים (*B'rei'shit bara Elohim*) effectively, I have one request: be prepared to set aside

---

[3]Why is בְּרֵאשִׁית בָּרָא אֱלֹהִים (*B'rei'shit bara Elohim*) awkward in Hebrew? Here is a concise, practical explanation. Translating *B'rei'shit* as "in the beginning" is problematic because of the Hebrew grammar. The word *B'rei'shit* is usually followed by a **noun**, not a verb. When a noun follows, the translation always includes "**of** " in English. The "of " emphasizes the special relationship between *B'rei'shit* and the **noun**. Consequently, we should translate בְּרֵאשִׁית בָּרָא אֱלֹהִים (*B'rei'shit bara Elohim*) in Genesis 1:1 as "In the beginning **OF** [He] created *Elohim*" or possibly "In the beginning **OF** creating *Elohim*." Both options are problematic.

[4]This is a famous song that was sung by the *Carpenters*.

familiar English translations of Genesis 1:1 to allow the Hebrew text to speak unhindered. Now, I have the second wonder: "In the beginning God created" **is an imprecise translation** for "בְּרֵאשִׁית בָּרָא אֱלֹהִים" (*B'rei'shit bara Elohim*). The **correct Hebrew translation** for "In the beginning God created" is "***B'rei'shit Elohim bara***" (בְּרֵאשִׁית אֱלֹהִים בָּרָא). For convenience, we will label this the *Pseudo Hebrew Version.* The **original Hebrew text of Genesis 1:1** is ***B'rei'shit bara Elohim*** (בְּרֵאשִׁית בָּרָא אֱלֹהִים). Notice that ***bara* and *Elohim* are switched**. This is extremely important. Take a moment to process. You may be saying, "David, I am stunned. I cannot believe the *Pseudo Hebrew Version* and the **original Hebrew text** are not identical! Why are they different? What is the **actual** English translation for ***B'rei'shit bara Elohim*** (בְּרֵאשִׁית בָּרָא אֱלֹהִים) if it is not 'In the beginning God created'?" Once again, a simple question requires a complex answer.

When you translate Genesis 1:1 strictly by the *chronology of the words* and adhere to the Hebrew grammar regarding ***B'rei'shit***, ***B'rei'shit bara Elohim*** should be translated as, **"In the beginning [He] created *Elohim.*"** (The "He" is *actually* God, the implied subject in the Hebrew word "*bara.*") On the surface, "**[He] created *Elohim***" might be perceived as a "heretical" interpretation (rendition), but it is also a literal translation![5] Perhaps this explains why standard versions read, "In the beginning God created"!

---

[5]At face value, how can God create *Elohim*? To avoid a potential heresy, **we must add brackets to**: "In the beginning [He] created *Elohim.*" The result is: "**In the beginning He** [the Absolute, Unknowable, and Unnamable God] **created** [the idea of knowing Him through the name of] ***Elohim***." The bracketed content discloses God's

Unfortunately, the name "*Elohim*" is lost. This is not acceptable because *Elohim* is the "All Powerful" Creator, and the name *Elohim* represents God's Attribute of Justice. Awkward Hebrew structures frequently lose their Hebraic meanings when translated into another language.

Before reaching a final translation, I must emphasize the **awkwardness** of the Hebrew grammar. We know that **God is the subject of Genesis 1:1.** If God is the subject, the Bible should have opened with the *name* of God–*Elohim*. When we pursue that thought, we discover **two** alternative structures that present God as the subject of Genesis 1:1. Version 1 is the unofficial *David Nekrutman Version* (DNV), which consists of an ordinary subject-verb format: ***Elohim bara b'rei'shit*** (אֱלֹהִים בָּרָא בְּרֵאשִׁית). ***Elohim*** (אֱלֹהִים) **begins** the verse and also serves as the **subject**. The main **verb** is the word בָּרָא (*bara*). Version 2–***B'rei'shit Elohim bara*** (בְּרֵאשִׁית אֱלֹהִים בָּרָא)–follows the same subject-verb structure, but the verse starts with ***B'rei'shit*** instead of *Elohim.* Version 3 is entirely different: "**בָּרִאשׁוֹנָה** בָּרָא" (***Ba'ri'sho'na bara***, At first, [He] created, Author's translation) fully replaces the awkward בְּרֵאשִׁית בָּרָא (***B'rei'shit bara***). ***Ba'ri'sho'na*** (**בָּרִאשׁוֹנָה**) is the mainstream, *uncomplicated* Hebrew term one would normally expect to appear. Table 20 contains the original Genesis 1:1 text and the three alternative versions we just discussed (see next page).

---

greater purpose. Humanity cannot fully know an infinite God. Through His gracious discernment, God created the idea of Himself through the name of *Elohim* to enable humanity to comprehend Him on an elementary level.

Table 20. Original Genesis 1:1 Text and Three Alternatives

Versions	Hebrew Text	Transliteration	English Translation
Common English Bibles			In the beginning God created the heavens and the earth
Original Hebrew Text	בְּרֵאשִׁית בָּרָא אֱלֹהִים אֵת הַשָּׁמַיִם וְאֵת הָאָרֶץ	***B'rei'shit bara Elohim et*** *ha'sha'mai'im v'et ha'a'retz*	**In the beginning [He] created *Elohim* the** heavens and the earth (Literal translation)
DNV 1	אֱלֹהִים בָּרָא בְּרֵאשִׁית	***Elohim bara b'rei'shit***	*Elohim* created at the beginning (Author's translation)
DNV 2	בְּרֵאשִׁית אֱלֹהִים בָּרָא	***B'rei'shit Elohim bara***	In the beginning, *Elohim* created (Literal translation)
DNV 3	בָּרִאשׁוֹנָה בָּרָא	***Ba'ri'sho'na bara***	At first, [He] created (Author's translation)

Overall, Table 20 illustrates our dilemmas concerning the Hebrew grammar. Notice the distinct arrangements of ***B'rei'shit***, ***Elohim***, and ***bara***. The secret to comprehending the table is to pay attention to the name *Elohim*. In the original Hebrew text, ***Elohim* is the third word** of the verse. This type of arrangement is awkward because *Elohim* never occupies the third position in the Hebrew Scriptures. For Version 1, God must have reasons for not accepting the *David Nekrutman Version* (DNV). Version 2 reads well in English, but the name ***Elohim* after *B'rei'shit*** is unacceptable in Hebrew! The Hebrew grammar does not allow a verb to follow ***B'rei'shit***. Version 3 is interesting, but it omits *Elohim*. We cannot conveniently delete the name of God. In the final analysis, none of the versions are acceptable. Is there another route? Definitely!

Readers and miners, our **only recourse** is clear: **we never tamper with God's grammar.** God purposely chose the structure, the Hebrew word *B'rei'shit*, and the Bible's specific word arrangement. Our task is to attempt to mine *what He wanted us to learn* from the Hebrew word *B'rei'shit* and the **original word order** of Genesis 1:1. So, miners there is a sign ahead: **Anagram Approaching**.

Welcome to Your First Biblical Anagram: B'rei'shit (בְּרֵאשִׁית) becomes Yirah Shabbat (ירא שבת)

Students, we have arrived at a crucial site. You will need the Jewish hermeneutics you just learned: **awkward words** prompt us to excavate, while **anagrams** enable us to uncover deeper insights from the text. By opening Genesis 1:1 with the **awkward** word *B'rei'shit* (בְּרֵאשִׁית) God was **alluding to** His original intention for the creation–*Yirah Shabbat* (ירא שבת)–Sabbath Awe. *Yirah Shabbat* is one of the most important nuggets in our *Shabbat* tour. **Through *Yirah Shabbat*, we realize that *Shabbat* is also a *time portal* for helping believers to**

> *Shabbat is a time portal to develop our awe of God, which biblically defines us as a human being.*

develop their sense of awe of God. (A time portal is the *scheduled training time* that *Shabbat* provides every week.)

Let me make a bold statement: **from a biblical perspective, a mature sense of awe for God is what defines a human being**. This is echoed by the wisest human being in the Hebrew Bible, King Solomon. Solomon authored the Book of Ecclesiastes and concluded his book with the following idea: a committed believer in God must pursue his or her internalization of **the awe of God** and obey His mandates because it is "the entire human being" (Ecclesiastes 12:13, Author's translation).

Miners, pay special attention to the phrase "the entire human being," because it is not a standard translation. The KJV says, "this *is* the whole *duty* of man," and the NIV reads, "for this is the duty of all mankind." I used "entire human being" because the Hebrew word for "duty" is not in the text. Wait! Somebody raised their hand. "David, *what* does 'the entire human being' mean; how did we get from awe of God to human being; and how did you find *Yirah Shabbat* in *B'rei'shit*?"

Those are fantastic questions! Let me respond by repeating: *Shabbat* is the *time portal* (conduit) for advancing *your* awe of God. Secondly, the biblical perspective in Ecclesiastes 12:13 helps shed new light on the meaning of *Shabbat*: **developing our sense of awe of Him transforms us into the inner essence of what it means to be a human being.** Finally, the concept of *Yirah Shabbat* is completely alluded to in the first word of the Bible—*B'rei'shit* (בְּרֵאשִׁית)—via **an anagram hermeneutic.**

Helping you excavate this *Yirah Shabbat* revelational nugget requires rearranging the letters in the first anagram in the Bible–בְּרֵאשִׁית (*B'rei'shit*). As your *moreh* (teacher), I will help you with the Hebrew letters.

The Hebrew word *b'rei'shit* contains six letters–*bet* (ב), *resh* (ר), *aleph* (א), *shin* (ש), *yud* (י), and *taf* (ת). The letters *yud*, *resh*, and *aleph* form the first word from the *B'rei'shit* anagram–***Yirah* (ירא)**. *Shin*, *bet*, and *taf* form the second word from the *B'rei'shit* anagram–***Shabbat* (שבת)**. Look at Figure 5:

Figure 5. ***B'rei'shit* to *Yirah Shabbat* Anagram**

The figure clearly illustrates how the anagram operates: **Two Hebrew letters are rearranged and a space is added—nothing is eliminated!** God did not choose His words from a thesaurus in order to impress His readership. Rather, He wants us to have a relationship with Him. The very first word of the Bible gives us a huge, revelational, relationship insight—**God's last creative act was His original intention—*Yirah Shabbat.*** Not only does a believer have the opportunity to soak in the Amplified Presence of God, *Shabbat* also provides us the time to reflect on how to become the human being God designed us to be.

You have successfully excavated the בְּרֵאשִׁית (*B'rei'shit*) anagram, but we should also mine **בָּרִאשׁוֹנָה (*Ba'ri'sho'na*)** for completeness. Remember, *Ba'ri'sho'na* (בָּרִאשׁוֹנָה) was the uncomplicated Hebrew term found in Table 20 (under DNV 3). Please check the table and refresh your memory. I will gladly wait for good miners.

When we excavate *Ba'ri'sho'na*, we see the "ש" and the "ב," but no "ת" (*taf*):

בָּרִאשׁוֹנָה (*Ba'ri'sho'na*)

[Notice that there's no ת (*taf*)!]

Unlike *B'rei'shit* (בְּרֵאשִׁית), *Ba'ri'sho'na* (בָּרִאשׁוֹנָה) does not contain the *Shabbat* anagram because the *taf* (ת) is missing. *Ba'ri'sho'na* also defies our two earlier nuggets: **1) God's last creative act was His original intention**, and **2) the Sabbath is God's creative masterpiece**.

Halleluyah! We just finished our current excavations. The mining and decoding revealed God's reasons for choosing *B'rei'shit bara Elohim*: the Bible is not a science book; it is a book about God's relationship with humanity and *Shabbat*. Therefore, **the first three words in the Bible should reflect relationship** rather than the sequence of God's creative actions. Consequently, **Genesis 1:1 must be translated as follows:**

The first three words in the Bible are about relationships.

"At the beginning of *Elohim* creating the heavens and the earth"
(Author's translation).

At the beginning of creating the world, God wanted humanity **to develop their awe of Sabbath**. God's last creative act was His original intention–*Shabbat*. Therefore, *Shabbat* has supremacy over the remaining six days. Once God created *Shabbat*, **all of the weekdays had to be rooted in the primary day–*Shabbat***. *Shabbat* represents a time when God ceased from His *weekday activities*. Likewise, **God invites us to enter His *Shabbat*, and *Shabbat* becomes the platform for how we act for Him during the week.** God accomplished unmatched, unrepeatable acts in six days, and we are expected to emulate Him. For six days we do and work, then we enter His Presence on the Sabbath. None of us will ever create as He did, but we can imitate Him in our actions. In a later excavation, you will discover how Genesis 1 and *Shabbat* reveal precisely what God asks us to do.

Notes

Chapter 14 Highlights

- All work must halt on the Sabbath because the Sabbath gives meaning for the week.
- *Bara* is the first verb of the Bible. It does not mean creation out of nothing.
- *Bara* expresses the ultimate *authority* of an object. Only God can "*bara*" something.
- We can be "*a'saer's*"—those who complete creation's final touches.
- The Hebrew word *Elohim* (or *elohim*) is plural and can refer to God, judges, angels, or pagan gods. Context determines the meaning of *Elohim* (*elohim*).
- *Bara* is singular. *Elohim* plus *bara* tells us that only *one* God created the world!
- Sabbath observance testifies that God is the Creator and Authority of all and affirms partnership with God for work (*a'sa*) during the week.

Your Sabbath Invitation

First the Sabbath, Then the Work

s human beings, our concept of time is connected to life. Today, we can access information on the Internet concerning "lifespan." The average lifespan is seventy-five years! We spend about twenty-six years sleeping and another six years eating. We spend another forty-three years dedicated to work and social activities. Now, Psalm 39 comes to mind, "'Show me, LORD, my life's end and the number of my days; let me know how fleeting my life is'" (v. 4 in most Christian Bibles; v. 5 in the Hebrew Bible). Each second of life is precious and offers an opportunity for us to sanctify time. **However, all work must reach a screeching halt when the seventh day arrives because the Sabbath establishes meaning for the other six days of the week.**

> *All work must halt on on the seventh day because the Sabbath provides meaning for the other days of the week.*

Understanding bara and a'sa

So far in Genesis 2:2, I have only explored the phrase "with the seventh day" without discussing the verb "had done (*a'sa*)." Before examining *a'sa*, I will go back to Genesis 1:1 to mine the verb *bara*. The word *bara* is the first verb in the entire Hebrew Bible. It not only precedes *a'sa* in the book of Genesis, but it also exceeds *a'sa*'s significance. The verb *bara* appears three times in the creation account of Genesis 1, as indicated in Table 21:

Table 21. *bara* in Genesis 1 (Author's translation)

Genesis 1:1	At the beginning of *Elohim* creating (*bara*) the Heavens and the earth
Genesis 1:21	And *Elohim* created (*bara*) the big *ta'ni'nim* (Leviathan or sea monster) and all living beings…
Genesis 1:26	And *Elohim* created (*bara*) the human being in His image…

Some commentators have focused on Genesis 1:1 to define *bara* as God creating something out of nothing and *a'sa* as God making something out of pre-existing material. **While the notion of God creating the world out of nothing may be true, it does not automatically and necessarily fit into the meaning of *bara*.** Aquatic life, sky life, and the human being (*Ha'Adom*) were created with the Hebrew term *bara*, but none of these were created "out of nothing." God fashioned each of them through existing material.

Yes, you can shout out, "Whoa, I never saw that coming!"

To underscore the point that *bara* does not necessarily mean "creating out of nothing," in Isaiah 41:20, *bara* appears within the larger context of restoration. The verse affirms that God will fulfill (*bara*) the restoration of Israel. The "*bara*" restoration of Israel that Isaiah describes does not transpire out of thin air. Rather, Israel's restoration manifests steadily through ongoing, tangible, historical events, which God Himself orchestrates.

Instead of conveying nothingness, I suggest **that *bara* expresses the ultimate authority of an object.** The first use of *bara* in the Bible occurs in Genesis 1:1 (see Table 21). The *bara* in chapter 1 of Genesis tells the reader that God is the Originator of all–from constructing the Heavens to forming all human beings. Here, let me affirm the magnitude of the word *bara*. The verb *bara* is conveniently rendered "created," but its true significance conveys "authority." In the entire Bible, the verb *bara* only applies to God. **God is the only One who can "*bara*" anything!** We will learn soon that all we can be is "*a'saers*" (completing the final touches of creation).

Bara expresses the authority of an object.

Look at Table 21. In verses 1:1, 21, and 26, Elohim *bara*'s "Heavens," "Leviathan," and "the human being." **Though the world is diverse, there is only one Creator.** As God-fearing Jews and Christians, we promptly say, "Amen," but the statement is colossal. The chief reason depends on the name of God given in Genesis 1:1–*Elohim*.

I am certain most of you are familiar with the name *Elohim*. With a capital "E" in English, *Elohim* refers to God the Creator. The term appears frequently throughout the Hebrew Bible, but **Hebrew does not have upper and lower-case letters.** *Elohim* with a lower case "e" can mean:

1. Judges
2. Angels
3. Pagan gods

The word "*elohim*" itself is a plural term in Hebrew. This is evident in Exodus 20:2, "You shall have no other gods (*elohim*) before Me." In Genesis 1:1, *Elohim* is capitalized in English because it does refer to God, and not gods. When translating this multi-functional word, how do we distinguish between "God" and "gods"? **Context is everything!**

In Genesis 1:1 the verb *bara* (create) helps us comprehend that *Elohim* should indeed be translated with a capital "E." **The magnitude of *bara* is like comparing Niagara Falls to water drops that trickle from your roof.** While *Elohim*, the Almighty name for God, exists in a plural Hebrew format, the verb *bara* is singular! The singular state informs us that **only one God created the world**–not a multiplicity of gods. Otherwise, if multiple gods were creating the world, then the plural word for *bara* would have appeared in the verse, namely the Hebrew verb *baru*–"they created."

*Only one God created the world because bara is a **singular verb**!*

When *Elohim* is mentioned in Genesis 1:1, we encounter the One with unmatched authority. This is why the first words in the Bible say, "*Bereshit bara Elohim*" or "At the beginning of Elohim creating (*bara*)" the Heavens and the Earth. Do you realize the audaciousness required to start a book with the declaration that God created everything? The Bible offers no apology or explanation. By God's own pronouncement, He initiates "creating" with the name "Elohim."

La'a'sot and a'sa

While *bara* conveys authority, **the verb *a'sa* emphasizes the completion of a process wherein the finishing touches are applied.** The best comparison I can provide for *a'sa* from the construction field is the Interior Decorator. Genesis 1 provides examples of God operating both as the Master Builder and as the Interior Decorator:

- Genesis 1:7–"So God made the vault and separated the water under the vault from the water above it. And it was so."
- Genesis 1:16–"God made two great lights–the greater light to govern the day and the lesser light to govern the night. He also made the stars."
- Genesis 1:25–"God made the wild animals according to their kinds, the livestock according to their kinds, and all the creatures that move along the ground according to their kinds. And God saw that it was good."

God completes the firmament process with the division of the waters, and He continues by adorning the solar system with the sun, moon, and stars. He also finalizes the species process for the wild beasts, domesticated animals, and for the living creatures that move slowly on the earth.

As I conclude, you should realize that the Sabbath observations in this chapter were developed from God's viewpoint:

1. God is the only One who is able to create through the Hebrew verb *bara*; human beings will never *bara* anything!
2. In Genesis 1:7, 1:16 and 1:25, God puts finishing touches on particular creations through the Hebrew verb *a'sa*.

In the context of *Shabbat*, God invites human beings to partner with Him and establish a relationship with their Creator through freedom of choice. **A celebration of the Sabbath not only testifies that God is the Creator and Authority of all, but affirms that its participants freely accept the responsibility to become God's partner. This partnership is manifested later during the week–via the verb *la'a'sot* (a form of *a'sa*)–but not on *Shabbat*.** Your "Yes" to the Sabbath Invitation means there is work ahead for you to do on behalf of God.

Shabbat participants freely accept partnership with God to do His work later during the week!

Notes

PART FIVE

A day to get excited about

Chapter 15 Highlights

- Sabbath partnership should never become artificial or exist for the sake of ritual.
- We renew our excitement for Sabbath partnership weekly by becoming a Sabbath Anticipator.
- "Sabbath Anticipator" is not in the Bible, but it is detectable in the Hebrew text of Genesis 26:5.
- Genesis 26:5 has five categories of regulations or "directives" that can be mined for revelation.
- "listened to My voice" is plain and unambiguous.
- "and he observed My charge" contains the Hebrew word שמר (*shomer*) in two forms.
- *Shomer* and *Shabbat* used together in other Bible passages yields translations of "*and he anticipated*" for "and he observed" and "*My Shabbat*" for "My charge."
- We can conclude that Abraham was a Sabbath Anticipator!

Your Sabbath Invitation

Sabbath Anticipation

In chapters 12–14, I explored Genesis 2:1–3 to unveil how God views the Sabbath. Together we learned and reinforced the following concepts:

Concepts

- God was always expecting humanity to celebrate the Sabbath.
- Sabbath is not ME time; Sabbath is HIS time.
- The creative act that manifested *with* the seventh day was the Sabbath.
- God is the only one who can *bara* anything.
- Humanity cannot *bara* anything.

- Sabbath is more than an ordinary invitation; Sabbath is a partnership with God.
- Sabbath is the spiritual tabernacle where one can connect with the Amplified Presence of God on that day.
- All weekdays should be rooted in the blessing and sanctification of God's Masterpiece–the Sabbath.
- When celebrating the Sabbath, we are not just declaring that God is the Creator. We are also accepting the partnership to *la'a'sot* (to fine tune) creation **only** during the weekdays.
- We never fine tune creation on *Shabbat.*

Each concept helped us to reconstruct our views of *Shabbat*. The concepts are products of acute Bible study, linguistic analysis, and orthodox Jewish exegesis. Essentially, we "mined revelation" utilizing the following interpretive principles:

Principles on How to Interpret Scripture

- There are no single-worded English terms to translate certain Hebrew expressions namely, *Shabbat*, *bara*, and *la'a'sot*.
- Frequently, **redundancies** in a biblical verse are platforms for excavating revelation.

At this point, let me pause and shout, "*Mazel tov*!" We have mined a lot of territory. Hopefully, you have embraced two specific concepts from above: **the Sabbath is more than an ordinary invitation**, and **the Sabbath is a partnership with God**. As we enter the next few chapters, I will introduce two additional concepts.

1. God gave general laws to humanity just after creation.
2. Abraham's family received specific laws from God, although such laws were not articulated as formal commands.

One of the core objectives in *Your Sabbath Invitation* is to reveal and illustrate that the Sabbath is a pre-Sinai celebration. Here, I am presenting both concepts as new additions, but they have always existed in *Your Sabbath Invitation.* To confirm this, in chapters 15–16, I will explore general laws, specific laws, and Abraham. My exploration involves three tasks: 1) examine some unique attributes of Abraham; 2) introduce the notion that our Patriarchs, Matriarchs, and other personalities "downloaded" the Torah prior to its written transmission at Sinai in Exodus 20; and 3) utilize the now familiar interpretive rule: redundancies in a biblical verse are platforms for excavating revelation. By the conclusion of chapter 15, you should comprehend that by celebrating *Shabbat* you are declaring to the world:

- The God of Abraham, Isaac, and Jacob is the Creator of the world.
- He is a merciful God.
- Time is Divine.

- *Shabbat* is God's Masterpiece.
- All of humanity will eventually celebrate *Shabbat.*

From Sabbath Partnership to Shabbat Anticipation

Any partnership may be exciting at the beginning, but after a while the initial enthusiasm begins to wane. **We never want our Sabbath partnership with God to become artificial, that is, a cooperation existing only for the sake of ritual**–one that is devoid of its original intention. A sacred day that declares God is the Creator of the world should never be transformed into a practice that borders on idolatry. For example, consider Isaiah 1:13:

> "Stop bringing meaningless offerings! Your incense is detestable to me. New Moons, Sabbaths, and convocations–I cannot bear your worthless assemblies."[1]

The verse above occurs in a time when Israel demonstrated faith outwardly, but inwardly, the people of Israel were assigning allegiance to the gods of other nations. The nation fulfilled the Sabbath routine but without God's true intentions for the day. Consequently, God responded

---

[1]God was not condemning the people for observing the Sabbath and the biblical festivals. He was condemning their lack of proper intent towards His appointed times.

by disassociating Himself from Israel. To avoid the trap of turning *Shabbat* into a meaningless ritual, **how can we constantly renew our excitement for the Sabbath partnership each week?** We do so by becoming a Sabbath Anticipator!

We renew our excitement for the Sabbath each week by becoming a ***Sabbath Anticipator****.*

As an avid traveler, I love watching people reunite with loved ones in the "Arrivals" section of the airport. The scenes are always energized, emotional, and saturated with ecstatic shouts, hugs, and tears. I can only imagine the preparations and errands the family member(s) faced and finished: cleaning the house, washing towels and sheets, buying the awaited traveler's favorite foods, and assembling a hefty welcome package in the guestroom. Some relatives even buy flowers, chocolates, or other small gifts to present at the airport. Ultimately, every gesture and activity is performed with joyful anticipation.

Before the arrival, the hours vanished leaving scant time to clean, shop, and to reorder the house. In contrast is the airport. The minutes drag by slowly as family members longingly wait for one individual to walk out of "Customs" and into "Arrivals." Finally, the precious face appears, and the anticipation deserved every moment! We need to treat *Shabbat* the same way!

Meet Abraham the First Shabbat Anticipator

Most of us know that Abraham lived a robust life of faith. We remember how God repeatedly tested Abraham's faith, under various conditions. For instance, God asked Abraham to leave his country and his father's house to journey to an unknown place (Genesis 12:1). In a different setting (Genesis 22:2), God directed Abraham to offer his son Isaac as a sacrifice. Abraham bound (*yaqada*) Isaac until God intervened by providing a ram in the thicket. Both accounts depict Abraham as he obeyed directives from God, and both fall under the first regulation category, which will be "excavated" below.

Both Jews and Christians admire Abraham's unshakable faith and obedience, **but how many of you recognize Abraham as the first *Shabbat* Anticipator?** The odds are few to zero because "*Shabbat* Anticipator" is absent from most English Bibles.[2] However, the term is detectable in the Hebrew text of Genesis 26:5:

> "Because that Abraham listened to My voice, and he observed My charge, My commandments, My statutes, and My laws" (Genesis 26:5, Author's translation).

Before excavating the Hebrew, we must understand the verse's setting. Genesis 26 transpires in Canaan, after another

---

[2]Search sixty-one English Bibles on BibleGateway.com to confirm!

famine has struck the region. Abraham had already died, "at a good old age," in Genesis 25:8. Years later, his son Isaac intends to leave Canaan (Genesis 26:1) and travel down to Egypt just as his father Abram (Abraham) had done in Genesis 12:10, "Now there was a famine in the land, and Abram went down to Egypt to live there for a while because the famine was severe." Anticipating this move, God appears to Isaac and says, "Do not go down to Egypt; live in the land where I tell you to live" (Genesis 26:2). Isaac listens to God, stays in the land, and relocates to Gerar, another city in Canaan (Genesis 26:6). As a reward for remaining in Canaan, God offers Isaac the land, future progeny, and the blessing of Genesis 12:3 (where God "will bless" nations through Abram). **Incidentally, God's abundant offers were not prompted by Isaac's merit, instead they are the result of Abraham's obedience.**

Occasionally, children are the beneficiaries of gifts bestowed on them after one or both parents have passed. Such gifts may stem from acts of kindness that the mother or father have performed for other people who lived during the same period. **Similarly, within the context of Genesis 26:1-5, Isaac is receiving Divine gifts based on the deeds that his father Abraham previously accomplished for God.** Genesis 26:5 reveals Abraham's deeds, which were listening to God's voice and obeying His commandments, statutes, and laws. In the end, Isaac becomes Abraham's primary beneficiary, and his only obligation is to remain in Canaan.

Without question, Abraham's obedience governs Genesis 26:5. Abraham's obedience is motivated and determined by a group of biblical regulations. According to Jewish exegesis, the verbal expressions in Genesis 26:5–"listened to My (God's) voice," "and he observed My charge," "My commandments," "My statutes," and "My laws"–have been classified into five different categories of regulations. Each category identifies a regulation or a "directive" that God gives to an individual. Moreover, biblical "directives" apply exclusively to people, not to any other segment of creation such as, animals, sea creatures, trees, or celestial bodies. In this chapter, we will only mine revelations for the first two directive categories: "**listened to My voice**" plus "**and he observed My charge**." I will address the last three directives in chapter 16.

Perhaps you remember my earlier desire to edit the Bible and to shorten Genesis 2:1–3. (See chapter 12.) Once again, if I were the editor, I would reduce Genesis 26:5 to, "Because Abraham listened to Me." Look at my version in Table 22:

Table 22. David's "Wishful" Version of Genesis 26:5

David's Version of Genesis 26:5	*God's Version of Genesis 26:5*
Because Abraham listened to Me.	Because that Abraham listened to My voice, and he observed My charge, My commandments, My statutes, and My laws.

Externally, my "Wishful" version succeeds because we still know Abraham listened to God. Internally, and more importantly, my rendition fails because it expunged the five directive categories: "listened to My Voice," "and he observed My charge," "My commandments," "My statutes," and "My laws." Thankfully, God is the Creator and the Designer of Torah, not me! He has a reason for including the five directives, even if they appear superfluous to me. So, I reject my version and apply the scriptural interpretive principle, "Redundancies in a biblical verse are platforms for excavating revelation."

Early in our journey, I explained that one cannot translate the word *Shabbat* as rest. *Shabbat* is *Shabbat*! *Shabbat* is a concept. Likewise, **when God tells Isaac that Abraham was obedient, He uses multiple directive categories to highlight the single word "obedience" because obedience is indeed a multi-faceted concept**. If God intentionally exaggerates Abraham's obedience, then His exaggerations demand our attention. Thus, **our excavation job in this chapter is to mine the regulation categories**. As the mining begins, please remember that Hebrew is read from right to left, and the English transliterations are read from left to right.

> *God uses multiple categories to describe Abraham's obedience.*

The First Two of the Five Directives

The five directives from Genesis 26:5 are listed on the next page in Table 23.

Table 23. Genesis 26:5: The Five Directives

Because that Abraham listened to My voice, and he observed My charge, My commandments, My statutes, and My laws.				
עֵקֶב אֲשֶׁר־שָׁמַע אַבְרָהָם בְּקֹלִי וַיִּשְׁמֹר מִשְׁמַרְתִּי מִצְוֹתַי חֻקּוֹתַי וְתוֹרֹתָי				
Ehkev asher shama Avraham b'koli va'yishmor mish'mar'ti mitz'vo'tai chu'ko'tai ve'toro'tai.				
וְתוֹרֹתָי	חֻקּוֹתַי	מִצְוֹתַי	וַיִּשְׁמֹר מִשְׁמַרְתִּי	אֲשֶׁר־שָׁמַע אַבְרָהָם בְּקֹלִי
ve'toro'tai	*chu'ko'tai*	*mitz'vo'tai*	*va'yishmor mish'mar'ti*	*asher shama Avraham b'koli*
and My laws	**My statutes**	**My command-ments**	**and he observed My charge**	**that Abraham listened to My voice**

"listened to My Voice"

The first directive category on the far right is "listened to My voice." The expression is plain and completely unambiguous; there are no hidden messages. Abraham followed explicit orders from God, per the aforementioned Genesis 12:1, "'Go for yourself, from your land, and from your relatives…'" and Genesis 22:2, "'bring him up there as an offering on one of the mountains I tell you.'" (Both are the Author's translations.)

"and he observed My charge"

The second directive is crucial because it fully explains how Abraham became a Sabbath Anticipator. The Hebrew for the second directive is וַיִּשְׁמֹר מִשְׁמַרְתִּי

(*va'yishmor mish'mar'ti*), and the translation we have been using is "and he observed My charge." When you examine the Hebrew of וַיִּשְׁמֹר מִשְׁמַרְתִּי (*va'yishmor mish'mar'ti*), and read from **right to left**, you will notice three common Hebrew letters in both words, a ש (*shin*), a מ (*mem*), and a ר (*resh*). Together, they form the word "שמר" (*shomer*). The word shomer is the first nugget from our excavation, and it enables me to translate *va'yishmor mish'mar'ti* as "and he anticipated My ***Shabbat***" in lieu of "and he observed My charge."

וַיִּשְׁמֹר מִשְׁמַרְתִּי

The Hebrew term *shomer* (**שמר**), within the framework of *Shabbat*, is found in the following passages. Each verse contains a form of the Hebrew word **שמר** (*shomer*) and the word **שבת** (*Shabbat*):

- Exodus 31:14–
  "'You should **observe** the **Sabbath** (**וּשְׁמַרְתֶּם אֶת־הַשַּׁבָּת**, *oo'shmar'tem et haShabbat*) because it is holy to you…'" (Author's translation).
- Exodus 31:16–
  "'Children of Israel shall **observe** the **Sabbath** (**וְשָׁמְרוּ בְנֵי־יִשְׂרָאֵל אֶת־הַשַּׁבָּת**, *ve'shamru B'nei Yirsael et haShabbat)* throughout their generations as an eternal covenant'" (Author's translation).
- Repetition of the Ten Commandments (Ten Categorical Statements) in Deuteronomy 5:12, "'**Observe** the **Sabbath** day

(שָׁמוֹר אֶת־יוֹם הַשַּׁבָּת, *shomor et yom haShabbat*), to sanctify it, as The Eternal your God commanded you'" (Author's translation).

- Isaiah 56:2–"'Fortunate is the person (*a'nosh*) that does this, son of man (*ben-adam*), that strongly grabs it, that **observes *Shabbat*** (שֹׁמֵר שַׁבָּת, *shomer Shabbat*) from profaning it, **and safeguards** (וְשֹׁמֵר, *veshomer*) his hand from doing any evil'" (Author's translation).
- Isaiah 56:6–"'And to foreigners who adhere to The Eternal, to minister to Him and to love the name of The Eternal, to become His servants–all who **observe** the **Sabbath** (כָּל־שֹׁמֵר שַׁבָּת, *kol shomer Shabbat*) from profanation, and who hold fast to My covenant'" (Author's translation).

By now you realize that one form of Jewish exegesis involves word studies and comparisons. A Hebrew word or phrase is compared and contrasted as it occurs throughout the Bible. The goal is to provide new revelation and to uncover potential Hebrew nuances. In the passages above, *shomer* and *Shabbat* appear together. In Isaiah 56:2, 6 the words appear shoulder to shoulder. **When words such as *shomer* and *Shabbat* occupy the same verse, Jewish commentators look for a potential relationship between the words**. If a sound relationship exists, fresh interpretations are uncovered, which commentators use to mine meanings in other passages. Therefore, any revelations we obtain from the *shomer-Shabbat* connections in Exodus, Deuteronomy, and Isaiah can be applied to the second directive in Genesis 26:5–וַיִּשְׁמֹר מִשְׁמַרְתִּי (*va'yishmor mish'mar'ti*). Let me walk you through the exegesis.

In the five verses above, the common phrase is "observe the Sabbath." (Isaiah 56:2 says, "observes Shabbat.") The phrase connects *shomer* (שֹׁמֵר) and *Shabbat* (שַׁבָּת). The second directive, *va'yishmor mish'mar'ti*, contains the word *shomer* (שֹׁמֵר) **twice**–which is more apparent in Hebrew: **וַיִּשְׁמֹר מִשְׁמַרְתִּי**. Next, apply *Shabbat* (**שַׁבָּת**) to *mish'mar'ti* (מִשְׁמַרְתִּי) based on the *shomer-Shabbat* connection. **The result is *mish'mar'ti* means "My Sabbath," though previously it meant "My charge."** Therefore, **the new translation for the second directive is "and he observed My Sabbath," as opposed to "and he observed My charge"**! Hallelujah! You just excavated platinum, and *Shabbat* just entered Abraham's world! Wow! The following equations explain our excavation:

*** Platinum Nugget Equations #1 ***

BEFORE EXCAVATION

***mish'mar'ti* = "My charge"**

AFTER EXCAVATION

***mish'mar'ti* = "My Shabbat"**

Your Sabbath Invitation readers, treasure the *platinum* for a few minutes because we still have another word to excavate–*va'yishmor*. The word *va'yishmor* is normally translated as "and he observed." **Our goal now is to demonstrate that *va'yishmor* = "and he anticipated."**

At the moment, you must have several questions, but there is **only one** that you should ask: 1) "Why did God choose the particular verb *va'yishmor* (and he observed) to emphasize Abraham's observance of Sabbath, as opposed to another verb such as קים (*ki'yim*), which means 'he fulfilled?' Then the verse would have said 'and he fulfilled My Sabbath.'" Readers, do not be surprised why I chose only one question because the **one** question is part of another *midrash*!

In English, the answer to the *midrash* is extremely obvious. The verb phrase 'and he observed' **is already** the perfect complement for the word "observance." **Quite the opposite, Jewish exegesis shouts, "No! Do not stop! Excavate further!"**[3] When we probe deeper, the first point we find is that *shomer* can also mean "anticipate."

Our first introduction that the root word *shomer* (שֹׁמֵר) means "anticipate" occurs in Genesis 37:5–11. There, Joseph reveals his dreams to his family that they will prostrate themselves before him. The reaction of Joseph's brothers was hatred and envy, "So his brothers envied him; his father **anticipated** (*shomer*) the matter" (Genesis 37:11, Author's translation). It seems that while Jacob was rebuking Joseph in front of the family, in his mind, he was anticipating the prophecy to be fulfilled.

---

[3]In chapter 8, recall the catchphrase "***midrash* answers the questions you should have asked**."

There are two other places in the Bible where *shomer* is translated as anticipate:

- Job 14:16–"But now, You count my steps; You do not anticipate (*shomer*) my sin" (Author's translation).
- Psalm 130:6–"My soul is to the Master among those who anticipate (*shomer*) the morning, those who anticipate the morning" (Author's translation).

If we apply the same exegetical techniques to *va'yishmor* that we did to *mish'mar'ti*, we acquire more platinum–**"and he anticipated," instead of "and he observed."** Below is the equation:

*** Platinum Nugget Equations #2 ***

BEFORE EXCAVATION

va'yishmor = **"and he observed"**

AFTER EXCAVATION

va'yishmor = **"and he anticipated"**

At last, when we merge the results of our excavations, the second directive from Genesis 26:5 becomes, "**and he anticipated My Sabbath**" or "**and he anticipated My *Shabbat*.**" The Patriarch Abraham, 400 hundred years before the events at Sinai, is a **Sabbath Anticipator**!

Conclusion for Chapter 15

Every word in the Bible has a purpose and meaning. Redundancies and word choices are opportunities for scriptural excavations that enable us to unlock a treasure trove of revelations. In this chapter, we explored the possibility of reducing Genesis 26:5 to "Because he listened to Me," but we rejected the idea because the verse connects Abraham's obedience to five Divine directive categories. Next, we defined two of the regulation (directive) categories: (1) listened to My voice; and (2) and he observed My charge.

> *Redundancies and word choices can unlock a treasure trove of revelations!*

The first directive category, "listened to My voice," covered outright requests from God such as, leaving everything behind to embark on an unknown destination journey (Genesis 12:1) to offering Isaac as a sacrifice (Genesis 22:1). In the second directive category, "and he observed My charge," we redefined the *va'yishmor mish'mar'ti* in Genesis 26:5 as "he was a Sabbath Anticipator." We excavated this treasure by completing several biblical, interpretative steps with the word *shomer*:

- We connected the Hebrew term *mish'mar'ti* to *Shabbat* in Exodus, Deuteronomy, and Isaiah.
- We joined the Hebrew term *va'yishmor* to the concept of anticipation through the stories in Genesis 26; Job 14:16; and in Psalm 130:6.

- We attempted to understand why God chose the verb *shomer* instead of the verb *ki'yim.*

More than just keeping the Sabbath, Abraham anticipated this sacred day.

In the next chapter, I will briefly define the three remaining directive categories. Then, get ready because I will shift to a topic that is less complicated and perhaps *fun*! Our Patriarchs, Matriarchs, and other biblical personalities were able to "download" the Torah prior to Sinai (Exodus 20). The ability to "download" the Torah before its public and physical manifestation at Sinai is directly connected to the Sabbath.

Notes

Chapter 16 Highlights

- "Download" is a Heavenly access of Torah before it was physically manifested at Sinai.
- Permission to download was given to Patriarchs, Matriarchs, and others who exercised faith in God the Creator. These biblical figures were not just esteemed persons, they were prophets.
- Abraham, Rebekah, and Joseph were provided access to the Heavenly Torah to intensify their relationship with God, and to equip them to help others grow closer to God.
- Abraham obeyed Divine commands that were both *explicit* and *implicit*. Without written instruction, Abraham knew how to pray, mourn, bury the dead, and tithe.
- Through "downloading," we can imagine that all of the Patriarchs, Matriarchs, and biblical figures celebrated *Shabbat* prior to its actualization at Sinai.

Your Sabbath Invitation

Downloading Heavenly Torah

In the previous chapter, we excavated and discussed two of the five directive categories from Genesis 26:5: "listened to My (God's) voice," "and he observed My charge." We used a familiar interpretive principle, "Redundancies in a biblical verse are platforms for excavating revelation." Our intense mining uncovered two platinum nuggets, which together revealed Abraham as the first *Shabbat* Anticipator. The three remaining categories are, "My commandments," "My statutes," and "My laws." These directives possess a peripheral connection to *Shabbat* because they only support Abraham as a Sabbath Anticipator indirectly. Therefore, we will not excavate them as we did the others in chapter 15. Instead, on the following page you will find concise definitions for the remaining directives in Table 24.

Table 24. The Last Three Directives in Genesis 26:5

Directives	Definitions	Biblical Support
My commandments	These directives are logical and reasonable from a human perspective.	The prohibition against murdering another human being (Genesis 9:6)
My statutes	Directives here lack human comprehension, reason, or explanation. God gives the order, and we humbly obey Him and fulfill His will.	Circumcision (Genesis 17:11)
My laws (*toro'tai*)	I redefined "laws" as "teachings." Such teachings embodied "learning process" moments, which God used to instruct Abraham how to internalize His Torah further.	a) God told Abraham to listen to Sarah regarding the Hagar incident (Genesis 21:12) b) God revealed to Abraham his destructive plans for Sodom and Gomorrah (Genesis 18:17, 28, 30, 32)

The directives above pertain to different facets of humanity, such as natural law (commandments–*mitzvot*), obedience (statutes–*choo-kot*), and learning moments (laws–*torah*).

One of the core objectives in *Your Sabbath Invitation* is to reveal and illustrate fresh concepts about the Sabbath. Thus, from the beginning, I have pursued the *why* of *Shabbat* so that you, the readers, would strongly consider accepting God's invitation to this sacred day. Early in chapter 1, I introduced a fundamental concept–one that sustains and energizes *Your Sabbath Invitation*: "Indeed, the Sabbath

Day predated the giving of the Torah at Sinai." In chapter 2, I presented a similar concept: "Although the giving of the Torah at Sinai occurred 3,500 years ago, the Heavenly Torah already existed prior to Exodus 20." Through the common phrase "giving of the Torah at Sinai," we learn that the inauguration of **the Sabbath Day** and the **"downloading" of the Torah** occurred prior to the events on **Mount Sinai**. Thus, in chapter 16, I will address the *fun* topic of **"downloading of the Torah" before Sinai** because the "download" is inextricably connected to *Shabbat.*

Obviously you will not find the Hebrew word "downloading" in the Hebrew Scriptures, but its contemporary meaning is a useful tool for explaining a somewhat esoteric concept. **When I use the word "download," I am referring to a Heavenly access of the Torah before it was manifested physically at Sinai.** Loosely, in computer terms, the Torah is in a virtual cloud awaiting someone with permission to "download" its priceless content. Within the context of *Shabbat*, **permission to download was available for our Patriarchs, Matriarchs, and other committed people** who exercised and maintained faith in God the Creator.

> *"Download" is Heavenly access to Torah prior to Sinai.*

To internalize this idea, it is important to review the revelation from chapter 2 of *Your Sabbath Invitation*. In that chapter, we learned that God created a Heavenly Torah, which He used to create the world. The Torah is earth's operating system. Although the written Torah was given formally at Sinai (Exodus 20), **its physical manifestation**

did not prevent anyone from accessing the Heavenly Torah via the Holy Spirit. In fact, there are several figures in the Book of Genesis who were committed to God and who qualified to access the Heavenly Torah. These biblical figures are not simply our esteemed Jewish ancestors–the Bible also identified them as **prophets**.

Several figures in the Book of Genesis were permitted to access the Heavenly Torah via the Holy Spirit.

For example, we usually remember Abraham as "the father of a multitude of nations," **but God called Abraham a prophet in Genesis 20:7**, when He ordered Abimelech to return Abraham's wife Sarah back to Abraham. When Rebekah is struggling to understand her severe labor pains, she went to seek The Eternal. God reveals to our Matriarch, "Two nations are in your womb" (Genesis 25:23). **God's revelation to Rebekah established her as a prophetess.** Lastly, before interpreting Pharaoh's dream, Joseph clarifies that God is the One who will provide answers for Pharaoh, not Joseph himself (Genesis 41:16). Thus, **Joseph is a prophet because God granted him the ability to discern heavenly matters** (prophetic dreams).

The Patriarchs, Matriarchs, and others committed to the Creator maintained a unique intimate relationship with God, which differed from the persons saturated in paganism. (See Genesis 41:8.) None of Pharaoh's magicians were able to interpret the dream, despite their tenacious efforts. **Evidently, God provided Abraham, Rebekah, and Joseph access to the Heavenly Torah to intensify their individual relationship with Him and to equip them to fulfill their**

respective ministries–ministries that helped others grow closer to God.

For the purposes of *Your Sabbath Invitation*, how does this lengthy discussion on the Patriarchs and Matriarchs relate to *Shabbat*? The answer repeats an earlier point: As righteous God-fearing individuals, Abraham, Rebekah, and Joseph accessed the Heavenly Torah before its transmission at Sinai. Each of these biblical characters obeyed implicit directives from The Eternal. **Therefore, we can conclude that they not only *accessed* the concept of *Shabbat*, but they also *practiced* the Sabbath before its actualization at Sinai.**

> *Abraham, Rebekah, and Joseph practiced Shabbat before it was actualized at Sinai.*

While the previous discussion highlights the Divine connections between the Heavenly Torah and the individuals who honor God, it also illustrates the benefits of following all of God's directives and commands, whether they are strongly declared or subtly implied. As Bible readers, you have probably encountered God's commandments and statutes prefaced with the imperatives "you shall" or "you shall not." However, there are several Divine directives that omit the familiar, explicit commands and, instead, will employ less obvious implicit ones. For example, **in the Hebrew Bible, God does not *outrightly* order us to pray, but we know prayer has biblical origins!**[1] Through a dream, God demanded king Abimelech to return Sarah to

---

[1]The notable verse 2 Chronicles 7:14 does not include a direct command from God ordering a human being to pray.

Abraham. **God also insisted that the king ask Abraham to pray for his recovery.** In Genesis 20:7, God declares, "And now return the man's wife, because he is a prophet, and he will pray for you and [you will] live. But if you do not return [her], know that you will surely die, you and all that is yours" (Author's translation).

First, God ordered Abraham "to pray" via his directive to Abimelech, which was not an *explicit* command to Abraham. **Second, the Scriptures exclude itemized instructions for Abraham about how "to pray"** for someone. The exclusion suggests that **Abraham already understood the charge "to pray"** and that God had asked him, at least once in the past, to pray for others.

*Abraham understood how to **pray** through a Heavenly download.*

A third example concerns burials and mourning. We all know that it is biblical to mourn and to bury a deceased person. However, you will not find an explicit mandate in the Hebrew Bible where The Eternal says, "Bury and mourn your deceased!" Yet, in the story of Sarah's death, we do find that Abraham purchased a burial plot, the Cave of Machpelah, and mourned for Sarah (Genesis 23:2). **Abraham could have performed the local Canaanite burial practices, but he followed a different course.** Abraham's choice must have been aligned with God.

*Abraham understood how to **bury and mourn** through a Heavenly download.*

Another example of a Divine directive prior to Sinai, which does not mirror an explicit commandment, is **tithing**. Genesis 14:21 shows **Abraham giving a tithe to Melchizedek before God issued His formal decrees in Leviticus**. On the other hand, there are several Divine directives that God clearly stated prior to Sinai such as, the charge to have children (Genesis 1:28), the prohibition concerning murder (Genesis 9:6), and the statute of circumcision God gave to Abraham (Genesis 17:11). Finally, God obviously knows that Abraham is commanding his household to "keep the way of The Eternal, to do righteousness (*tze'da'kah*) and justice (*mishpat*)" (Genesis 18:19, Author's translation).

*Abraham understood how to **tithe** through a Heavenly download.*

As I conclude, let me summarize the goal for this chapter: to demonstrate that **biblical characters who were committed to God the Creator were able to access (download) the Heavenly Torah, in order to implement various commandments and directives into their lives.** Therefore, through "downloading," it is not difficult to imagine that *Shabbat* was still celebrated by all of the Patriarchs, Matriarchs, and other Bible figures, prior to its initial written form at Mount Sinai. **After all, *Shabbat* is God's masterpiece, and God intended all humanity to celebrate the sacred day.**

Notes

Chapter 17 Highlights

- In the Genesis 26:5 directives, the noun in *mitz'vo'tai* is *mitzva*, "commandment." In *toro'tai* the noun is *torah*, "teaching."
- A Divine directive must be introduced to be actualized. *Mitzva* has an underlying rationale. *Torah* is internalized.
- *Shabbat* celebration belongs to the *mitzva* category.
- God supplied heavenly bread for food in the Sin Desert. As a faith test, twice as much was gathered on the sixth day, and none was gathered on *Shabbat*.
- In Exodus 16:23, God declares the rare expression "*Shabbaton Shabbat*" without providing instructions for *Shabbat*.
- Despite Egyptian enslavement, the Jewish people celebrated the *mitzva* of *Shabbat* that was downloaded to their ancestors.
- *Shabbat* incorporates the idea of trusting God as the ultimate Source of our life provisions.

Your Sabbath Invitation

The Shabbat of Shabbatot

"And Elohim said, 'This is what The Eternal declared:
"Tomorrow is a Shabbaton Shabbat
holy to The Eternal..."'"

Exodus 16:23 (Author's translation)

In chapter 16 we learned that our Patriarchs, Matriarchs, and other biblical characters, who were committed to God in the Book of Genesis, were able to download the Torah prior to Sinai. In chapters 15-16, we studied the different categories of Divine directives in Genesis 26:5: "that Abraham listened to My (God's) voice (*asher shama Avraham b'koli*)," "and he observed My charge (*va'yishmor mish'mar'ti*)," "My commandments (*mitz'vo'tai*)," "My statutes (*chu'ko'tai*)," and "My teachings (*toro'tai*)." I presented these directives using the possessive case of the noun. For example, *mitz'vo'tai* is "My commandments," but the noun itself is *mitzva*, which means "commandment." Likewise, *toro'tai* is "My teachings," but the noun in the word is *torah*, which means "teaching." I am highlighting the grammar so that we can probe the *mitzva* and *torah* directives a bit further in this chapter.

Before I transition into a new *Shabbat* revelation, let me finalize the idea of "accessing the Heavenly Torah" and its connection to *Shabbat*. The following primers will help you process the revelations we are going to excavate from Exodus 16:

- One can only actualize a Divine directive **after** that directive has been introduced into the life of a person or community.
- The Hebraic week consists of seven days, and the Egyptian calendar followed a ten-day week.
- While they were slaves in Egypt, the children of Israel probably conformed to the Egyptian calendar.
- Although slaves, the children of Israel never forgot the tradition of *Shabbat*.
- The category of *mitzva* is a Divine directive with an underlying rationale.
- *Shabbat* celebration belongs to the *mitzva* category.
- The category of *torah* is a Divine teaching from God that must be internalized by a person or community.

A month after the Exodus from Egypt, the Jews found themselves without food or water in the Sin Desert (Exodus 16:1). In response to their complaints about the lack of sustenance, God promises to provide them heavenly bread. However, God adds a caveat "'…And the nation (*ha'am*) should go out and gather a day's portion every day, that I may test them as to whether they will abide by My law (בְּתוֹרָתִי, *b'torati*) or not. And it will come to pass on the sixth day that they shall prepare that which they bring in, and it shall be twice as much as they gather daily'" (Exodus 16: 4–5, Author's translation).

The heavenly bread is a test of faith from God. The test requires a person to leave their dwelling and gather the bread each day. The *torah* teaching concerning this act of faith is that there is no such thing as "stocking the shelves." The people had to learn complete reliance on God for everyday provisions. The **additional** *torah* teaching is that the people were required to collect a double portion on the sixth day because **no** heavenly bread would be provided on *Shabbat*. The faith test had two expectations: 1) Collect **a double portion on Friday**–believing God provided sufficient bread for Friday and *Shabbat*, and 2) **Do not attempt to gather or find any** heavenly bread **on the seventh day**.

When the sixth day arrived, the tribal leaders informed Moses that everyone had collected a double portion (Exodus 16:22). Moses responds,

> And *Elohim* said, "This is what The Eternal declared: 'Tomorrow is a *Shabbaton Shabbat* (שַׁבָּתוֹן שַׁבָּת) holy to The Eternal. What you are going to bake, bake; what you are

> going to cook, cook. All that is leftover, put aside for yourselves to keep until morning'" (Exodus 16:23, Author's translation).

The people left the heavenly bread until the morning of *Shabbat*, and it was still fresh and free of worms or maggots! Moses, then says to the people, "'Eat today since it's *Shabbat* today to The Eternal. Today, you will not find [the heavenly bread] in the field'" (Exodus 16:25, Author's translation).

The Hebrew expression *Shabbaton Shabbat* is only mentioned once in the Hebrew Bible, in Exodus 16:23. Table 25 provides the Hebrew text and its transliteration:

Table 25. Exodus 16:23

וַיֹּאמֶר אֲלֵהֶם הוּא אֲשֶׁר דִּבֶּר יְהוָה שַׁבָּתוֹן שַׁבַּת־קֹדֶשׁ לַיהוָה
Va'yo'mare Elohim hu asher de'bare Adonai Shabbaton Shabbat kodesh la'Adonai

Normally, the expression is in the reverse order–*Shabbat Shabbaton*–and is connected to two holidays, *Shabbat* and the Day of Atonement (*Yom Kippur*), as well as the Sabbatical Year (*Shmita*).[1]

---

[1]Regarding *Shabbat*, the expression appears in Exodus 31:15 (*Shabbat Shabbaton*); 35:2 (*Shabbat Shabbaton*); and Leviticus 23:3 (*Shabbat Shabbaton*). About the Day of Atonement, *Shabbaton Shabbat* appears in Leviticus 16:31 (*Shabbat Shabbaton*) and 23:32

One way of translating the rare *Shabbaton Shabbat* expression in Exodus 16:23 is as follows: **“And *Elohim* said, ‘This is what The Eternal declared: “Tomorrow is a *Shabbaton* (a cessation period) [for you, which is a] *Shabbat kodesh* to The Eternal…”’” (Author’s translation).**[2]

At this point, forgive me, but I must interrupt this exciting narrative with an extremely important question. **Where did Moses receive the instruction that the seventh day was *Shabbat*?** If you examine the verses in chapter 16 prior to verse 23 you will find that God said nothing to Moses regarding *Shabbat*. If I were standing next to Moses at the time, I would have asked him, “What is a *Shabbat*?” **Obviously, the people already understood the concept of *Shabbat*.** Otherwise, Moses would have instructed the people about *Shabbat* and then proceeded with the heavenly bread instructions.

> *Moses and the people must have already understood Shabbat because no Sabbath instructions were given to them.*

Surprisingly, after centuries of slavery in Egypt and working in accordance with the Egyptian ten-day calendar

---

(*Shabbat Shabbaton*). The expression of *Shabbat Shabbaton* is found when the Bible discusses the Sabbatical Year in Leviticus 25:4.

[2]Many Bible translators render the word *kodesh* as “holy” or “sanctified.”

week, **the Jewish people never lost the *mitzva* of *Shabbat* that was downloaded by their ancestors Abraham, Isaac, and Jacob**. With the Divine *torah* teaching concerning heavenly bread, the people needed to internalize the notion of full dependence on God for sustenance. Moreover, full dependence entailed trusting God that the double portion collected on the sixth day would last through *Shabbat*. The task sounds elementary from our modern perspective, but the children of Israel were just redeemed from slavery, which included absolute reliance on taskmasters for daily food and water. **The mandate to trust God exclusively was an unfamiliar and monumental undertaking.**

> *Despite their Egyptian slavery, the Jewish people never lost the mitzva of Shabbat downloaded by their ancestors.*

In Exodus chapter 16, Sabbath is elevated from 1) a celebration of God the Creator, 2) the pipeline to the original merciful act God bestowed on humanity, and 3) the acknowledgment of a partnership between God and humanity, to an additional dimension. **Now, Sabbath incorporates the idea of trusting God as the ultimate Source of our life provisions.** *Shabbat* becomes the training ground for learning resolute trust in Him.

Notes

PART SIX

A day for all humanity

Chapter 18 Highlights

- Exodus 16 contains two "community" terms: "children of Israel" (*b'nei Yisrael*) and "the nation" (*ha'am*).
- Non-Israelites exited Egypt with the Jewish people. They are included in "the nation."
- The non-Israelites celebrated *Shabbat* with the Jewish people on the seventh day.
- The non-Israelites first appeared in Exodus 12:38 as the "great mixed multitude."
- The seventh day was identified by Divine revelation to Moses. Exodus 16 is the first chapter in the Bible where the seventh day is named as *Shabbat*.
- In Exodus 16, for the first time in Scripture, a multiethnic group of human beings is operating in a Sabbath manner.
- *Shabbat* is not just a Jewish experience. God desires all human beings to celebrate *Shabbat*.

Your Sabbath Invitation

The Nation Celebrates Shabbat

Often, when we discuss the Exodus from Egypt, we relegate the story solely to the children of Israel (***b'nei Yisrael***), the descendants of the House of Jacob. Seldom do we realize that non-Israelites also exited from Egypt with the Jewish people. We will begin our excavation with the account found in Exodus 16. I will provide the passages for you:

> Yet on the seventh day, some of the people from the nation [wish] to gather [the heavenly bread]; they found none. The Eternal said to Moses, "How long will you refuse to keep My commandments (*mitz'vo'tai*) and My laws (*ve'toro'tai*)? See that The Eternal has given you the *Shabbat*: therefore, He gives you on the sixth day two days' [worth of] bread! [Let] every man remain in his own place! Do

> not go out from your place on the seventh day!" So the nation (הָעָם, *ha'am*) *shabbated* on the seventh day (Exodus 16:27–30, Author's translation).

In Exodus chapter 16, you will notice two "community" terms–"children of Israel" (*b'nei Yisrael*) and "the nation" (*ha'am*). They appear in the following verses:

- "The entire congregation of the children of Israel (***b'nei Yisrael***) complained against Moses…" (Genesis 16:2, Author's translation).
- "The Eternal said to Moses: 'Behold I will cause to rain bread from heaven for you; and the nation (***ha'am***) will go out and gather each day's portion on that day…'" (Genesis 16:4, Author's translation).
- "And when the children of Israel (***b'nei Yisrael***) saw [the heavenly bread], they said to one another, 'What is it?'…" (Genesis 16:15, Author's translation).
- "Yet on the seventh day, some of the people from the nation (***ha'am***) [wish] to gather [the heavenly bread]; they found none" (Genesis 16:27, Author's translation).
- "So the nation (***ha'am***) *shabbated* on the seventh day" (Genesis 16:30, Author's translation).

Non-Israelites are actually included in the term "the nation" (***ha'am***). Moreover, if we examine the account again, we will discover one particular moment prior to Sinai where everyone celebrated *Shabbat*: "So the nation (***ha'am***) *shabbated* on the seventh day" (Exodus 16:30, Author's translation). The phrase "*shabbated* on the seventh day" means "the nation celebrated *Shabbat*."

Once again, I am discerning a possible question from you: "David, how do you know that 'non-Israelites' are included in 'the nation' because Exodus 16 seems to focus on the 'children of Israel'"? My answer: "I will show you." The non-Israelite people who experienced the Exodus *with* the children of Israel in Exodus 16 first appeared in Exodus 12. Table 26 identifies these non-Israelites as the "great mixed multitude" (עֵרֶב רַב, *erev rav*).

Table 26. Exodus 12:38 (Author's translation)

"And also, a **great mixed multitude** went up with them, and sheep, and oxen—an abundance of livestock."	וְגַם־עֵרֶב רַב עָלָה אִתָּם וְצֹאן וּבָקָר מִקְנֶה כָּבֵד מְאֹד *V'gam erev rav o'lah e'tom v'zon oo'ba'kar mik'neh ka'ved m'od*

The "great mixed multitude" included a combination of non-Israelite slaves, Egyptian citizens, mercenaries, and other non-Israelites that intermarried with the Israelites.[1] This means that a group of non-Israelites went out of Egypt

[1]I determined the members of the "great mixed multitude"(עֵרֶב רַב, *erev rav*) by examining different portions of Scripture. For example, we know that **non-Israelite slaves** were imprisoned during the Firstborn Plague in Exodus 12:29. It is obvious from Exodus 12:38 that **Egyptian citizens** also exited Egypt with the Jewish people. The verse

and anchored their fate with the Jewish people. Furthermore, these non-Israelites *shabbated* with the Jewish people on the seventh day.

Take a moment to internalize Exodus 16:30, "the nation *shabbated* on the seventh day," because the only parallel to this phrase in the Hebrew Bible is "[*Elohim*] *shabbated* on the seventh day" (Genesis 2:2, Author's translation). Table 27 compares the phrase in Exodus 16:30 and Genesis 2:2 (next page).

Table 27 portrays definite similarities between the two verses. In Exodus 16:30, the only way the people knew that it was the seventh day was by Divine revelation. God had informed them through Moses (Exodus 16:23, 25). Remember, at this point, the nation (the children of Israel

---

states, "And also, a great mixed multitude went up (עָלָה, *o'lah*) with them…" (Author's translation).

Concerning **the Egyptian mercenaries**, their presence can be deduced from Exodus 13:18, "So *Elohim* led the nation via the desert road toward the Sea of Reeds. The children of Israel were armed (חֲמֻשִׁים, *cha'mu'shim*) when they went up from Egypt" (Author's translation). The Hebrew term "*cha'mu'shim*" may also signify mercenaries as opposed to Israelites themselves bearing arms. Therefore, it is also possible that a **mercenary army** accompanied the Israelites. So, an alternative reading of Exodus 13:18 would be the following: "So *Elohim* led the nation via the desert road toward the Sea of Reeds. The children of Israel were accompanied by [non-Jewish] mercenaries when they went up from Egypt" (Author's translation).

Another group are people who **intermarried with the children of Israel, which would include Egyptians and other non-Jewish residents**. For example, in Leviticus 24:10 we find a family with an Israelite woman married to an Egyptian man. Thus, I contend that at the time of Exodus 16, the "great mixed multitude" consisted of Egyptian royalty, regular Egyptian citizens, immigrants who lived in Egypt, and former slaves from other parts of the Egyptian empire.

Table 27. Exodus 16:30 and Genesis 2:2 (Author's translations)

Exodus 16:30	Genesis 2:2
וַיִּשְׁבְּתוּ הָעָם בַּיּוֹם הַשְּׁבִעִי	וַיִּשְׁבֹּת בַּיּוֹם הַשְּׁבִיעִי
va'yish'b'tu ha'am ba'yom ha'sh'vi'e	*va'yish'boat ba'yom ha'sh'vi'e*
So the nation ceased (*shabbated*) on the seventh day.[2]	And He [*Elohim*] ceased with the seventh day.[3]

and the mixed multitude) were still accustomed to the Egyptian calendar, which consisted of a ten-day week. **Although *Shabbat* was already known after humanity was created** (Genesis 2:3), **Exodus 16 is the first chapter in the Bible where we see the seventh day named as *Shabbat*** (Exodus 16:23, 25, 26). In fact, God gave several specific *Shabbat* directives to the people:

- Collect a double portion on Friday (Exodus 16:22)

---

[2]Remember, in the Exodus 16 story, some people violated the Sabbath by attempting to gather additional heavenly bread. Once the nation is rebuked, the people finally *shabbated* on the seventh day. Nevertheless, the story occurs **on** *Shabbat*. For this reason, I translated *ba'yom* as "**on** the" as opposed to "**with** the."

[3]Regarding Genesis 2:2, God does not create anything **on** *Shabbat*; He does not *bara* anything **on** *Shabbat*. God literally creates *Shabbat* on the twilight **between** the sixth day and the seventh. This clarifies why I translated *ba'yom* as "**with** the" in Genesis 2:2 instead of "**on** the." God *shabbated* "**with** the" *Shabbat* instead of "**on** the" *Shabbat*. God never violated His own *Shabbat*.

- Prepare *Shabbat* food on Friday (Exodus 16:5, 23)
- Purposely leave some of the heavenly bread collected on Friday for *Shabbat* (Exodus 16:26, 29)
- Don't leave your home to attempt to gather the heavenly bread on *Shabbat* (Exodus 16:26, 29)

> *For the **first** time in Scripture, we are witnessing a **multiethnic** group of human beings operating in a Sabbath manner!*

All the Divine directives above center on food. Although God had provided enough sustenance on *Shabbat*, some individuals violated God's directive by leaving their homes to search for more heavenly bread. After the reprimand from God, both the children of Israel and the mixed multitude–*ha'am*–finally '*shabbated*' (Exodus 16:28–29). **Right here, for the first time in canonized Scripture, we are witnessing a multiethnic group of human beings operating in a Sabbath manner.** The message from the study in this chapter is that ***Shabbat* is not just a Jewish experience. God desires all human beings to celebrate *Shabbat*!**

Notes

Part Seven

You are cordially *invited* . . .

Chapter 19 Highlights

- This chapter contains practices to be prayerfully considered that you may adopt to amplify your *Shabbat* experience.
- A *minhag* (plural, *minhagim*) is a Jewish religious practice to spontaneously demonstrate devotion and loyalty to God.
- *O'neg Shabbat* relates to your best culinary dishes and beverages.
- *A'shet Chai'yil* (normally translated "a woman of valor") is a title that was only given to Ruth.
- Ephraim and Manessah became the children of Jacob.
- *Shabbat* practices remind us of our role in advancing redemptive history.

Practical Advice for Shabbat Beginners

Praise The Eternal One! This is the last chapter of *Your Sabbath Invitation*, and it is positively the most requested chapter. Many who are reading this book already practice a form of *Shabbat* and zealously longed to glean new tips, activities, and recipes from me. Nevertheless, my goal from the start was to explain the *why* of *Shabbat* thoroughly, as a response to Isaiah 66:23. The beginning of *Your Sabbath Invitation* stated, "I will show you that behind all the conversations and apart from all the commotion, a peaceful scenario exists. I will explore Isaiah 66:23 and demonstrate that Sabbath observance is directly related to the end of time, and the coming of the messiah (Messiah)." Thus, to adopt *Shabbat* practices without an accurate Scriptural understanding would nullify my original intent. Instead, I prayed extensively and meticulously layered numerous Hebraic concepts so that you would consider adopting the Isaiah 66:23 prophecy into your life. In fact, the first "callout" box declared, "A meaningful Sabbath is brewed and voluntary. It is NOT instant coffee!" In addition, "Time and deliberate actions are prerequisites for understanding the Sabbath *and* for implementing Sabbath celebrations with awe."

Faithful readers, the "*why* of *Shabbat*" is finally concluded. Chapter 19 now offers a template for the "***how* of *Shabbat*,**" but do not panic. **This chapter does not include a list of "do's and do not's" concerning what you can and cannot do on *Shabbat*.** You are **not** suddenly obligated to buy or bake *challah* each week, a special Eastern European braided bread that many Jews still eat today on *Shabbat*. Neither do I expect you to savor gefilte fish, a poached mixture of ground deboned carp, whitefish, or pike, combined with horseradish and a carrot. (The culinary medley tastes much better than it sounds!) Furthermore, you will not be required to adopt the Jewish practice of reading select chapters from the Pentateuch and the Prophets, known as *Pa'ra'shat Ha'sh'vu'ah* and *Haf'ta'rah*.

Do not panic!
This chapter does not contain a list of "do's" and "do not's" regarding Shabbat.

Unfortunately, we do not have a canonized biblical text or written records outlining the *Shabbat* celebrations of our Patriarchs, Matriarchs, and other figures in Genesis. **Nonetheless, the Jewish people have continued to be faithful stewards of *Shabbat* for the last 3,300 years.** The founder of cultural Zionism and famous Hebrew essayist

Asher Zvi Hirsch Ginsberg (1856-1927), pen name *Ahad Ha'am*, once remarked, "More than the Jewish People have kept *Shabbat*, *Shabbat* has kept the Jews."[1] **Numerous *Shabbat* practices introduced and exercised by Jewry toward the end of the Second Temple Period and into the Middle Ages, I still observe today.** In fact, many Christians who have eaten at my *Shabbat* table have been inspired to implement similar practices in their own homes.

Many Christians have been inspired to implement similar Shabbat practices.

Therefore, I have chosen certain practices which you may prayerfully consider and perhaps adopt in your own Sabbath celebrations. Technically, some of my choices qualify as Orthodox Judaism's comprehensive approach to *Shabbat*, such as "**Remembering *Shabbat* During the Week.**" In a New York minute let me revisit the parameters I wrote in chapter 1: "[A]s an Orthodox Jew involved in the sacred calling to advance Jewish-Christian relations, I do not expect you to convert to Judaism or practice Judaism's customary approaches to the Sabbath. **Instead, I desire for you to view Sabbath as an attractive integral part of a godly lifestyle.**" Now the circle is complete because the stipulations from chapter 1 have been fully realized in chapter 19. **All of the practices outlined in the final chapter of *Your Sabbath Invitation* are intended to amplify your *Shabbat* experience not to impose requirements!**

---

[1]*Ha'Shi'lo'ach*, vol. 3, no. 6 (May 1898): n.p., https://lib.cet.ac.il/pages/item. asp?item=7147/ (14 September 2021).

Minhag

Before I explain the distinct *Shabbat* and pre-*Shabbat* traditions, I have one more delay. We must examine the *why* of the "how of *Shabbat*." "David, I thought we finished the *why* component of *Your Sabbath Invitation*." We certainly did, but *why* still precedes *how*, especially now! So, I am introducing another concept–*minhag*.

The term *minhag* is usually translated as "custom"; however, as you might expect, the English translation does not accurately represent the concept. First, *minhag* (מנהג) is from the root *nahog* (נהג) which means "to lead."[2] **A *minhag* was a religious practice established by our Jewish ancestors to spontaneously demonstrate devotion and loyalty to God.** A *minhag* could emerge from an individual, family, or an entire community, and its influence could exceed its original source. For example, a *minhag* conceived by one small family could be adopted by Jews in another city or country. The *minhagim* (plural for *minhag*) "reflect the enduring vitality and eternal freshness of the religious impulse, the unbroken creativity of our people, and its continued prophetic strength."[3] Earlier, I used the word "spontaneously," but a *minhag* is not the result of a whim or momentary impulse. Rather, **in the lived experience of the *Shekinah*, the individual, family, and**

---

[2]Abraham Chill, *The Minhagim: The Customs and Ceremonies of Judaism, Their origins and Rationale.* 2nd edition (Sepher-Hermon Press: New York) xix.

[3]Joseph Kalir, "THE MINHAG," *Tradition: A Journal of Orthodox Jewish Thought* 7, no. 2 (1965): 90, https://www.jstor.org/stable/23256064/ (25 June 2021).

community were moved to protect or deepen the spirituality of *Torah*.[4]

> *Shabbat Minhagim demonstrate our love for God and our eagerness to be in His Amplified Presence.*

Our love for God always exceeds our mere attendance at a scheduled encounter. Our love also includes the smaller tasks and actions we perform daily, which communicate to God: "Father, we cannot wait for our weekly reunion with You." ***Shabbat Minhagim* demonstrate our eagerness to be in the Amplified Presence of God on the Sabbath.** Some of the traditions below are true *minhagim*; others are exclusive Jewish *Shabbat* practices, and some function in both categories. So, refill your coffee mugs, water bottles, or tumblers because the **first practice** in *Your Sabbath Invitation* has arrived. The activity is easy and requires no equipment.

Remembering Shabbat During the Week

Shabbat occurs on one day, but every day prepares the way for *Shabbat*. Each day is an opportunity to remember and to demonstrate to God that we are looking forward to His Amplified Presence and to connecting with Him in a more profound manner, without the chaos of the week. To augment your *Shabbat* anticipation, turn the page to Table 28, where I have supplied declarations for you to recite daily.

---

[4]See Glossary for "lived experience of the *Shekinah*."

Table 28. Daily *Shabbat* Declarations

Sunday	*Hayom yom rishon b'Shabbat*! Today is the first day of *Shabbat*!
Monday	*Hayom yom shei'ni b'Shabbat*! Today is the second day of *Shabbat*!
Tuesday	*Hayom yom sh'li'shi b'Shabbat*! Today is the third day of *Shabbat*!
Wednesday	*Hayom yom r'vi'e b'Shabbat*! Today is the fourth day of *Shabbat*!
Thursday	*Hayom yom cha'me'shi b'Shabbat*! Today is the fifth day of *Shabbat*!
Friday	*Hayom yom shi'shi b'Shabbat*! Today is the sixth day of *Shabbat*!
Saturday	*Hayom yom Shabbat kodesh*! Today is the Holy *Shabbat*!

Table 28 contains the transliterated Hebrew on top and the corresponding English translation below. I recommend that you declare them in Hebrew! *Lamah lo*? (Why not?)

O'neg and Ka'vod Shabbat

Presently, as students of *Your Sabbath Invitation* and of the Bible, you know that Isaiah 66:23 inspired this book. In the verse, the prophet envisions a day when all of humanity will be celebrating *Shabbat*. Pages ago, I mentioned the primary reason Isaiah merited the prophecy.

Isaiah permitted heathens, who had abandoned their idolatrous pasts and who were now believing in the God of Israel, to be a part of the Jewish community (Isaiah 56:3). One indication of their faith in the God of Israel was their observance of *Shabbat*. Isaiah had witnessed an Exodus 16:30 moment: both Jews and non-Jews were *Shabbating* together.

> *The book of Isaiah both opens and closes on the topic of Shabbat.*

***Shabbat* is a bookend for the beginning and the end of biblical Isaiah.** The sacred book opens with the prophet's rebuke because the nation of Israel was not applying its heart to observe *Shabbat*. The Book of Isaiah concludes with the now familiar Isaiah 66:23 prophecy where all of humanity is celebrating *Shabbat*. Moreover, Isaiah transforms *Shabbat* to another level by introducing the concepts of *O'neg Shabbat* and *Ka'vod Shabbat* in Isaiah 58:13:

> If refrain your foot from breaking *Shabbat*, from pursuing your affairs on My *ka'dosh* day, if you declare ***o'neg*** (עֹנֶג) to *Shabbat*, the holy [day] of The Eternal shall be ***m'choo'bod*** (מְכֻבָּד), and if you ***v'chi'bad'toe*** (וְכִבַּדְתּוֹ) by not going your own way, pursuing your own affairs or speaking a word (Author's translation).

The first Hebrew term Isaiah presents is *o'neg* (עֹנֶג), commonly translated as "delight" or "pleasure." Once again, we have a Hebrew term that lacks a one-word English equivalent. No other day in the week, biblical holiday, or commandment is associated with the concept of *o'neg*. Furthermore, the verse is instructing one to **declare** *Shabbat* **as** *o'neg* because *Shabbat* itself is **not** *o'neg*. The term *o'neg* in Isaiah is related to food and drink:

> "Attention! All who are thirsty, go to water, and whoever has no money, go, buy and eat, and go, buy without money and without a price, wine and milk. Why should you weigh out money without bread and your efforts without satisfaction? Listen, listen to Me and eat what is good, and your soul shall delight (*o'neg*) in fatness" (Isaiah 55:1-2, Author's translation).

Based on the uniqueness of *o'neg* in its relation to a Divine mandate and on *o'neg*'s distinct connection to food and drink, Jewish tradition has excavated the following revelation: **one should purchase and enjoy special *Shabbat* cuisine**.[5] Furthermore, all the preparatory activities, such as shopping and cooking the food during the weekdays can be elevated to an *O'neg Shabbat* status.

> *Transform your grocery shopping into an O'neg Shabbat experience.*

Yes, you understood me correctly. **Anyone can transform their grocery shopping experience into *O'neg Shabbat*.** Imagine walking into a grocery store with a smile and the

---

[5]Babylonian Talmud Shabbat 119a.

cashier asks you, "Why are you so happy?" Your response is, "I was on an *O'neg Shabbat* shopping spree!" From filet mignon to your favorite coffee, such items can be elevated to an *O'neg Shabbat* status by simply declaring these groceries as "for *O'neg Shabbat*." Boiling water, beating the eggs, filleting fish, dicing vegetables, frying chicken cutlets, seasoning salmon, baking the bread, rolling the sushi, caramelizing sugar, and other cooking activities associated with your *Shabbat* culinary dishes can be elevated to the status of *O'neg Shabbat*. **Enjoy your favorite culinary delights on *Shabbat*!**

Another significant aspect of Isaiah's transformation of *Shabbat* is the notion of *Ka'vod Shabbat*.

> ...the holy [day] of The Eternal shall be *m'choo'bod* (**מְכֻבָּד**), and if you *v'chi'bad'toe* (**וְכִבַּדְתּוֹ**) by not going your own way, pursuing your own affairs or speaking a word (Isaiah 58:13, Author's translation).

Notice the bold font for the three Hebrew letters "*kaf*" (**כ**), "*bet*" (**ב**), and "*da'let*"(**ד**). The word *ka'vod* (**כבד**) is usually translated as "honor." The term is mentioned twice in the verse. The first *ka'vod* (**מְכֻבָּד**, *m'choo'bod*) **signifies that the day itself requires honoring**, and the second *ka'vod* (**וְכִבַּדְתּוֹ**, *v'chi'bad'toe*) **relates to activities that people should not do** on *Shabbat*.

Overall, we have learned that *Shabbat* provides emancipation for the soul, a spiritual elevation, and a more amplified communion with The Holy One blessed be He.

Furthermore, ***Shabbat* is viewed as an opportunity to enter into God's Kingship**. Therefore, to "*ka'vod Shabbat*" means to treat this day **as if we are hosting a king in our home**. We would definitely wear our finest clothing and our homes would be immaculate. Just as *O'neg Shabbat* incorporates preparatory activities, *Ka'vod Shabbat* follows likewise. Doing the laundry, ironing, shining our shoes, sending the suit or dress to the dry cleaners, sweeping, vacuuming, dusting–even showering–are all opportunities to elevate to *Ka'vod Shabbat*. All of these activities are part of the **first *ka'vod*** in Isaiah 58:13.

Shabbat is an opportunity to enter into God's ***kingship****; we treat the day as if we are hosting a* ***king****.*

As I mentioned previously, the second *ka'vod* in Isaiah 58:13 relates to activities that should **not** be done on *Shabbat*–"by not going your own way, pursuing your own affairs, or speaking a word" (Author's translation). *Shabbat* is the opportunity to reflect on our spiritual walk with God as an individual, family, and community. The Sabbath is not a personal day to reflect on our careers, homework assignments, and individual goals. It is not a ME day! ***Shabbat* is a HIM day!** In the next section we will examine one of the three activities mentioned in Isaiah 58:13 under the second וְכִבַּדְתּוֹ (*v'chi'bad'toe*)–our speech.

Shabbat Speech

The "speaking a word" portion of Isaiah 58:13 is partly self-explanatory. The phrase does not denote a vow of silence. Instead, it signifies redirecting the words we speak to the level of *Shabbat* speech.[6] Our *Shabbat* conversations should be different from our weekday discussions. On *Shabbat*, God ceased the creative speech acts that He had accomplished during the six weekdays. Similarly, a human being should cease his or her speech from worldly matters.[7] ***Shabbat* is an opportunity to reflect on the power of speech.**

Words matter and the Bible does not promote or condone the right to the Freedom of Speech, particularly malevolent speech. God not only mandates us not to slander one another (Leviticus 19:16), but Solomon also warns, "death and life are in the hand of the tongue" (Proverbs 18:21, Author's translation). The Talmud asks, "Does the tongue have a hand?"[8] Proverbs and the Talmud inform us that the tongue is able to kill just as a hand kills. The famous children's rhyme that claims "sticks and stones may break my bones, but names will never hurt me" is biblically wrong.

The concepts of *O'neg* and *Ka'vod Shabbat* appear immediately after Isaiah is pleading with the nation of Israel to improve their moral behavior and to end the interpersonal gossip:

> Then you will call, and The Eternal will answer; you will cry, and He will say, 'Here I am.' If you remove perverse conduct from

---

[6]Babylonian Talmud Shabbat 113b.

[7]Jerusalem Talmud Shabbat, Venice ed., Ch. 15, Law 3; Jerusalem Talmud Shabbat, Vilna ed., 78a.

[8]Babylonian Talmud Arachin 15b.

> your midst, the pointing of the finger, and malicious talk (Isaiah 58:9, Author's translation).

Shabbat empowers us to discover the **power** of **positive speech**.

While we are familiar with the prohibitions against gossip, slander, defamation of character, and other forms of malicious speech, ***Shabbat*** **empowers us to discover the power of positive speech** which encourages our family members and verbally supports members of our community. This matter concerning words and speech is an ideal segue for the next practice: preparing biblical communications for the Sabbath.

Preparing Shabbat Biblical Messages

Scripturally charged subjects discussed at the Sabbath table enhance relationships with God.

The first recommended practice consisted of *Shabbat* declarations to raise your Sabbath anticipation throughout the week. Another practice functions likewise, but it entails work. **Fortunately, the favorable results surpass the required work: prepare scripturally charged subjects and messages to be discussed at the Sabbath table. The Friday evening conversations should enhance our relationship with God.** Bear in mind that *Shabbat* is not a retreat from family, friends, or the community. Sabbath celebrations enrich our covenantal homes and communal life through *predetermined* dialogues and teachings designed to transform our character and to revitalize (hone, improve) our social interactions. In addition, the Bible studies themselves elevate our knowledge of God and His Word. The *Shabbat* meals are an organic way to internalize all of these biblical discussions, as we break bread and fellowship together.

Accepting Shabbat Earlier

Strictly speaking, the Sabbath begins Friday evening at sunset–the exact moment the seventh day begins. However, **one should never initiate *Shabbat* precisely at sunset!** When we start the Sabbath **before** the mandated time, **we attest to God our anticipation** to enter His Amplified Presence, rather than our endeavor to do what is minimally required. Effectively, our early start changes the sixth day's minutes into *Shabbat*.

The notion of human beings transforming moments from the sixth day into *Shabbat* is deduced from what is missing in Genesis 2:1–3. In Genesis 1, every verse that mentions a weekday, (Genesis 1:5, 8, 13, 19, 23, and 31), contains the phrase "It was evening, and it was morning" (Author's translation), but the verses for the seventh day (Genesis 2:2–3) omit the phrase.

> *What is missing can be as important as what is stated in the text.*

There is a Jewish hermeneutic that asserts: **what is missing can be as important as what is stated in the text**. We are missing "It was evening, and it was morning" regarding the seventh day. God did not accidentally forget to insert this creational pattern, which appears with every other day of the week in Genesis 1. A possible revelation to explain why God intentionally omitted "It was evening and it was morning" is the following golden nugget: **God bestows the Divine license for human beings to convert moments from the sixth day and form them into *Shabbat*.**

Process this for a moment! Truthfully, *Shabbat* exists and occurs–week after week–whether we are prepared or not. Yet, there is an aspect of the Sabbath in which we can actively participate without waiting for the exact "God" moment to arrive. **We can add time to Sabbath**. By doing this, we are accomplishing the *Imitatio Dei*, walking in His ways (Deuteronomy 28:9). **Not only are we Sabbath Anticipators, in effect, we are also Sabbath Innovators!**

> *We are both Sabbath Anticipators and Sabbath Innovators!*

Adding time to the Sabbath expresses, "God, we value and love our relationship so much that we are willing to meet with You earlier than expected." Just as God created the world with His word, we too can declare "God, I am adding *ka'dosh* to the weekday and I accept the Sabbath." **True Sabbath affection begins with adding time.**

The Inauguration of Shabbat in the Home

If you have seen films or pictures related to *Shabbat*, they often depict women lighting candles to inaugurate *Shabbat* in the homes of Jewish people. The custom of lighting *Shabbat* candles originated in the late Second Temple Period and is sourced from Isaiah 58:13 in order to fulfill the ***o'neg* and *ka'vod*** of *Shabbat*. The *Shabbat* candles provide a special ambiance to the household (*ka'vod*). Pragmatically, having light in the home allows you to enjoy your meal (*o'neg*) and prevents you from stumbling around in the dark! Although homes today have electric lights, Jews have continued the custom of lighting designated *Shabbat* candles.

Prior to lighting the *Shabbat* candles and to fulfill Isaiah 58:10, practically, we perform the *minhag* of depositing money in a charity box: "When you offer your soul to the hungry, and you satisfy the starving creature…" (Author's translation). Today, you can accomplish the same *minhag* before lighting the candles by donating online to the poor.

After lighting the candles, some maintain a custom of praying to God with the following liturgical prayer, which precedes spontaneous personal supplications:

> May it be Your will, Lord my God and God of my fathers, to be gracious to me and members of my family; grant us good and long life; remember us for good and blessing; consider us for salvation and compassion; bless us with great blessings; make our household complete, crowning our home with the feeling of Your Divine Presence dwelling among us. Make me worthy to raise learned children and grandchildren, who are wise and understanding, who love and fear God, people of truth, holy and attached to God, who will dazzle the world with Torah and goodness and service of God. Please hear our prayers, in the merit of our

> matriarchs Sarah, Rebecca, Rachel and Leah, and ensure that the glow of our lives will never be dimmed. Show us the glow of Your face and we will be saved. Amen.[9]

The point is that one should strive to create a special *Shabbat* ambiance and enjoyment by using the light.

Shabbat Liturgy

Liturgy is an important aspect of the *Shabbat* experience. Every Friday evening, we use liturgy to welcome *Shabbat*. From the start, we have studied Genesis 2:1–3, Psalm 92, and Isaiah 66:23 rather extensively, and any combination of these texts would be ideal *Shabbat* texts to recite at the Sabbath table. Naturally, you are free to create your own melodies to accompany the recitations.

A'shet Chai'yil —A Woman of Valor?

I hope you have detected a steady rise in the complexity of the Sabbath practices and *minhagim*. The next two traditions may be particularly appealing and meaningful to wives and children**, but they are also extremely relevant to every participant**. The first *minhag* is the ***A'shet Chai'yil***, pronounced with a **long** "*A*." As a Jewish husband, the ***A'shet Chai'yil*** is a tremendous blessing because it allows me to revitalize my marriage at least fifty-two times a year. **If you are participating in *Shabbat* and you are not a husband or wife, be encouraged because you are still**

---

[9] "Candle Lighting," Aish.com, n.p., n.d., http://image.aish.com/candles.pdf.

honoring the original intention of this *minhag* by paying homage to the Amplified Presence of God–the *Shekinah*, and His Torah.

Every Friday evening at the *Shabbat* table, husbands sing a love song to their wives–Proverbs 31:10–31, the *A'shet Chai'yil* (אֵשֶׁת חַיִל).[10,11] While we are not trying to croon like Frank Sinatra or Michael Bublé, we do intend to honor our wives and to let them know we truly appreciate them. Proverbs 31:10 asks the question, "*A'shet Chai'yil*, who can find?" When we sing the verse, the answer is already in front of us–our wives. The words *A'shet Chai'yil* appear in the beginning of the verse:

אֵשֶׁת־חַיִל מִי יִמְצָא וְרָחֹק מִפְּנִינִים מִכְרָהּ

(*A'shet Chai'yil mi yim'tza v'ra'choq mip'pi'nim mich'rah*)

"*A'shet Chai'yil* who can find?
For her value far exceeds pearls"

(Proverbs 31:10, Author's translation)

The recitation of *A'shet Chai'yil* on Friday evening was introduced sometime in the middle of the sixteenth century as a way to greet God's Amplified Presence on *Shabbat* and to express verbal gratitude to God for giving us His Torah.[12]

---

[10]Some of have transliterated *A'shet Chai'yil* as "*Eshet Chayil*" or "*Eshes Chayil.*"

[11]Notable translations of *A'shet Cha'yil* include: "a woman of valor," "a virtuous woman," "a worthy woman (or wife)," "excellent wife," and "a wife of noble character."

[12]See Shemu'el Pinhas Gelbard, *Rite and Reason: 1050 Jewish Customs and Their Sources* (Mifal Rashi Publishing: Petach Tikvah, 1998), 276.

In my research, I could not determine the exact date the *A'shet Chai'yil*'s *minhag* umbrella was enlarged to include the twenty-two verse, acrostic poem portion of Proverbs 31, for the purpose of honoring wives.[13] **Regardless, the beauty of *minhag* dynamics is that the original intention does not limit the *minhag*'s future potential.** Later communities of faith, generations removed, can discover new revelations and usher the *minhag* to a deeper level. *Midrashically*, *A'shet Chai'yil* is the pronoun which represents the *Shekinah* and the Torah.[14] Briefly, *Shekinah* is the feminine aspect of God. Both the *Shekinah* and the Torah are feminine words. Thus, because Torah was given on *Shabbat*, and *Shekinah* is the Amplified Presence of God, which is augmented on *Shabbat*, *A'shet Chai'yil* represents Torah and the *Shekinah*. **The Proverbs 31:10 question containing the words *A'shet Chai'yil* refers to Torah and to the *Shekinah*.**

My brief explanation is especially important to anyone who is single: **The *minhag A'shet Chai'yil* recitation is always sung on *Shabbat*, whether one has a wife or not,**

---

[13]Ronald L. Eisenberg, *Jewish Traditions: JPS Guide* (The Jewish Publication Society: Philadelphia, 2004), 129.

[14]According to the Babylonian Talmud Shabbat 86b, the Torah was given on *Shabbat*. Further discussion exceeds the limits of *Your Sabbath Invitation* to understand how the *midrash* connected *A'shet Chai'yil* to the *Shekinah* and to the Torah, both personified as a woman (Midrash Proverbs 31:2). There is a *midrash* that claims Proverbs 31:10-31 was Abraham's eulogy of Sarah. (Consider https://www.sefaria.org.il/Midrash_Tanchuma_Buber%2C_Chayei_Sara.3?lang=bi). My *midrashic* contention is that via the Holy Spirit, Bathsheba downloaded *A'shet Chai'yil* and advised her son, King Solomon, on the importance of finding a wife.

because its original institution was to greet His Amplified *Shabbat* Presence and to exhibit our gratitude for the Torah. So, **men and women**, if any of you are single by choice or through varied life circumstances, singing opportunities *still* exist! **We need you to serenade the *Shekinah* and the Torah on *Shabbat*!** Naturally, after a man becomes married, he looks at his wife passionately and professes, "You are my *A'shet Chai'yil*."

> *The A'shet Chai'yil was originally instituted to greet God's Amplified Shabbat Presence and to exhibit gratitude for the Torah.*

By now, did you notice that I have not translated the phrase *A'shet Chai'yil*–the first two words of Proverbs 31:10? My avoidance is intentional. The expression only appears in Ruth and Proverbs:

1. Ruth 3:11–"And now my daughter, do not be afraid; all that you said I will do. Since all the gate of my nation knows you are an ***A'shet Chai'yil*** (אֵשֶׁת חַיִל)" (Author's translation).
2. Proverbs 12:4–"***A'shet Chai'yil*** (אֵשֶׁת־חַיִל) is a crown to her husband; but like rot in his bones, a shameful one" (Author's translation).
3. Proverbs 31:10–"***A'shet Chai'yil*** (אֵשֶׁת־חַיִל) who can find? For her value far exceeds pearls" (Author's translation).

Before we examine *A'shet Chai'yil* further, you must understand some historical information about Ruth and Proverbs. Sequentially, the book of Ruth is the **eighth book** in most contemporary Christian Bibles (Catholic, Protestant, and Greek Orthodox). Ruth follows the Book of Judges and precedes the Book of 1 Samuel. Ruth's placement is almost reversed in the Hebrew Bible because **Ruth** follows Proverbs and precedes the Song of Songs, but it lies **near the end of the Hebrew Bible** (*Tanakh*).[15] According to Jewish tradition, Samuel the prophet authored the Book of Ruth and Solomon is the author of Proverbs.[16] (Unlike Joshua, Ruth did not author her own book.)

The Book of Ruth transpired during the period of the Judges, a time of moral chaos when everyone was doing "as they saw fit in their own eyes" (Judges 21:25, Author's translation). By contrast, the Book of Proverbs was composed in an era of complete peace during the kingship of Solomon. The name Solomon (שְׁלֹמֹה, *Shelomo*) means "peaceable" because it is derived from the Hebrew word for peace–שָׁלוֹם (*shalom*). Many of you know that Ruth is the great-grandmother of Solomon, but **did you know the King**

[15]The Hebrew Bible consists of twenty-four books divided into three sections: the *Torah* (Instruction/Law), the *N'vi'im* (Prophets), and the *K'tu'vim* (Writings). Most contemporary Protestant Bibles contain the same books, but they subdivide the twenty-four books into thirty-nine. For example, Jews treat the *Torah* as one book, but Christians count the same material as five books (Genesis, Exodus, Leviticus, Numbers, and Deuteronomy) Sequentially, Ruth lies in the middle of *K'tu'vim*, which is the third section of the *Tanakh* (Hebrew Bible). By the way, *Tanak* is an acronym for *Torah*, *N'vi'im*, *K'tu'vim*.

[16]See Babylonian Talmud Bava Bathra 14b-15a regarding Samuel and the Song of Songs Rabbah 1:8 concerning Solomon.

Lemuel in Proverbs 31:1 is Solomon? The name Lemuel means "belonging to God." Interestingly though not uncommon for Jews, Solomon had several names: "Yedidyah," "Kohelet," "Ben Yakah," "Agur," and Lemuel.[17] In Proverbs 31:10–31, King Solomon is recording his mother's advice on the qualities of a godly wife. The *A'shet Chai'yil* expression **only occurs three times in the Hebrew Scriptures and is uniquely associated with the Davidic line**. That being said, the expression is primed for major revelational excavation, so you know what I expect you to do: come mine *A'shet Chai'yil* with me.

On its own, the Hebrew word *a'shet* means "wife of" or "woman of" (Genesis 11:29; Exodus 20:13); but *chai'yil* has several meanings:

- In the context of army service: "valiant" (Judges 18:2, 20:44)
- In the context of spiritual empowerment: "strong" (2 Samuel 22:33)
- In the context of financial well-being: "wealth" (Deuteronomy 8:18)

Ruth is the only woman in the Bible ever to receive the A'shet Chai'yil appellation.

Biblically, the only woman ever to receive the *A'shet Chai'yil* appellation is Ruth–"And now my daughter, do not be afraid; all that you said I will do. Since all

[17]See Avot d'Rebbe Natan (39:4).

the gate of my nation knows you are an *A'shet Chai'yil*" (Ruth 3:11, Author's translation).

Circumstantially, if we recall what Ruth endured to join Israel, and according to the honorable definitions above, we should translate *A'shet Chai'yil* literally as "a virtuous woman" or "a virtuous wife." Yet, within the context of the story, does Ruth really qualify as an *A'shet Chai'yil*? She was not Wonder Woman, General Issue (GI) Jane, or a soldier serving an elite unit of the Israel Defense Forces. Economically, Ruth was a poor widow collecting the leftover gleanings in the fields of Bethlehem. The Bible does not record a spiritual or emotional crisis that Ruth powerfully overcame. In fact, Naomi was more emotionally distraught than Ruth!

All the same, Ruth has three outstanding deeds in her favor: 1) she abandoned her idolatrous Moabite past; 2) she vowed to commit to Israel's God (Ruth 1:16-17); and 3) she voluntarily decided to help Naomi (Ruth 2:1). **Ruth's actions are irrefutably noble, but they hardly render her an *A'shet Chai'yil*.** Is there another message *A'shet Chai'yil* conveys? Does *A'shet Chai'yil* perform a specific function?

A leading theme in Ruth is "identity."

The answer to both questions depends on a leading theme found in Ruth–**identity. Identity is the metaphorical protagonist** in Ruth.[18] As a Moabite, Ruth

[18]A protagonist is the primary character in a book, story, movie, drama, or narrative and is occasionally regarded as the hero or heroine. The term "metaphorical protagonist" is reminiscent of a similar phrase in chapter 9, "Adam's Defense Attorney": "Of the two subjects,

is a descendant of the nation that refused hospitality to Israel and that attempted to curse Israel during their days in the wilderness (Deuteronomy 23:4). As a result of these offenses, a Jew cannot marry a Moabite (Deuteronomy 23:3). Throughout the Book of Ruth, the narrator and others in the story **identify** Ruth as "Ruth the Moabite" or "Moabite." However, **two people who speak directly to Ruth never mention her identity–Naomi and Boaz.** In fact, Naomi and Boaz call Ruth "my daughter." On the other hand, Boaz continues to recognize her as a Moabite when speaking to others. Is Boaz a hypocrite or an ashamed, two-faced man? Absolutely not! Boaz simply identifies Ruth as others do in the community.

Table 29 on the following page depicts several identities for Ruth from five different sources. As mentioned earlier, "The Author of Ruth" is the prophet Samuel. Samuel's designations for Ruth are broad, objective, and **conventional**. Skip momentarily to the last three portions. Predictably, Naomi uses the affectionate title "my daughter" while the Head Reaper only says "Moabite." It is interesting that "daughter-in-law" is used solely by Samuel and the women.

Boaz echoes Samuel's formality and Naomi's endearing "my daughter." His "my daughter" in Ruth 3:11 is especially unusual when he says, "And now my daughter, do not be afraid; all that you said I will do. Since all the gate of my nation knows you are an *A'shet Chai'yil* (אֵשֶׁת חַיִל)." Keep

---

Shabbat functions as the metaphorical main character in Psalm 92. *Shabbat* is the masterpiece in God's creation." Whereas *Shabbat* is the *metaphorical* masterpiece in Psalm 92, identity is the *metaphorical* champion in the Book of Ruth.

Table 29. Various Ways Ruth is Identified in the Book of Ruth

The Author of Ruth	
…identifies Ruth as "Ruth"	1:14, 1:16, 2:8, 4:13
…identifies Ruth as "Ruth the Moabite"	1:22, 2:2, 2:21
…calls Ruth "daughter-in-law"	1:6, 1:11, 1:22, 2:22
…identifies Ruth as a "Moabite"	1:4
Boaz when speaking	
…directly to Ruth calls her "my daughter" (and never "Ruth the Moabite" or "Moabite")	2:8, 3:10, 3:11
…to the kinsman, identifies Ruth as "Ruth the Moabite"	4:5
…to the elders, identifies Ruth as "Ruth the Moabite"	4:10
Naomi	
…identifies Ruth as "my daughter"	1:11, 1:12, 2:22, 3:1
The Head Field Reaper	
…identifies Ruth as "Moabite"	2:6
The Women	
…identify Ruth as "daughter-in-law"	4:15

in mind that our primary goal is to comprehend *A'shet Chai'yil*. To do this, we must understand the phrase the first time it appears in the Hebrew Bible. The initial occurrence is in Ruth 3:11, which determines the meanings of *A'shet Chai'yil* in Proverbs 12:4 and 31:10.

When we consider Ruth 3:11, many translators are perplexed by the phrase "all the gate of my nation" (*kol sha'ar a'mi*, כָּל־שַׁעַר עַמִּי). The KJV states, "all the city of my people" and the NIV reads, "All the people of my town." Both versions sound correct. Apparently, the phrase mirrors a contemporary public opinion poll, so in the vernacular of Ruth's day, *kol sha'ar a'mi* means, "Everyone in the city knows you are an *A'shet Chai'yil*." Such gossip is flattering and is hardly libelous. **If that is the case, why did Boaz instruct his people to make certain no one harassed Ruth (v. 2:9)? Why badger an *A'shet Chai'yil*?** In fact, Boaz was the only one who exercised compassion towards Ruth by providing her abundant food and exclusive access to his silos. In the setting of the story, no one cared about the Moabite widow, Ruth, and her mother in-law Naomi–the woman who left the city during a food crisis.

*A'shet Chai'yil is Ruth's **new identity** resulting from her acceptance into the Jewish community.*

Readers, I suggest that "all the gate of my nation"[19] is completely unrelated to the locals who are amazed at Ruth's virtuous behavior. Instead, **the rare term reflects a Holy Spirit vision** which foretells Boaz of Ruth's eventual acceptance into the community of the Jewish people. **The *A'shet Chai'yil* is Ruth's new identity as a member of the Jewish community and represents the loss of her Moabite tribal status.** *A'shet Chai'yil* only occurs **three times** in the Hebrew

[19]The only other time *sha'ar ami* appears in the Hebrew Scriptures is in Micah 1:9 in reference to Jerusalem.

Scriptures, and the term is uniquely associated with the **Davidic line**. Both *A'shet Chai'yil* and *kol sha'ar ami* enter the Hebrew Scriptures for the first time in Ruth 3:11. Thus, I firmly assert that their simultaneous debut in Ruth 3:11 **is not a coincidence.** Together, these facts are prime conditions for a major excavation!

As students of the Book of Ruth, we are fully acquainted with the narrative, so Boaz's reactions to Ruth are not surprising. Now, for a few moments, pause and reread the story slowly as it unfolds, or approach the Book as if it were your first encounter. I propose that there are two chief ways for the story to evolve: (1) Boaz reacts in anger and curses Ruth for her promiscuous behavior; or (2) Boaz willingly violates the moral code of God and engages in an intimate act with Ruth, hoping no one ever exposes the indiscretion. However, a plot twister occurs in the following poetic dialogue (Ruth 3:9–11, Author's translation):

Boaz: Who are you?

Ruth: I am Ruth, your handmaid. Spread your skirt on your handmaid for you are the redeemer.

Boaz: May you be blessed by The Eternal. Your last *chesed* is better than your first–not to follow young men whether rich or poor. And now my daughter, do not be afraid; all that you said I will do. Since all the gate of my nation (*kol sha'ar ami*) knows you are an *A'shet Chai'yil.*

When reading this dialogue, you can see the Divine hand of God! **Boaz realizes that Ruth is not intending to have a one-night fling. Ruth desires to be redeemed.**

Overall, Ruth's actions are the opposite of her Moabite background:

- She journeys with Naomi to Israel.
- She embraces the God of Israel.
- She feeds Naomi.
- She does not remarry.
- She accepts Naomi's undercover mission to be alone with Boaz in the middle of the night, knowing that the consequences of her actions might go awry.
- She expresses to Boaz the need to be redeemed.

A person who identifies as a Moabite would never perform any of these actions!

I suspect that many of you are quite familiar with the biblical mandate of a **Levirate marriage**, although you may not recognize its technical title. The Levirate marriage results when the brother of a deceased man marries his brother's widow. This particular marriage is mandated in Deuteronomy 25:5–10. **As a Moabite widow, Ruth is not required to fulfill Torah law, but she still feels the need to continue the name of her Jewish husband Mahlon, and her mother in-law Naomi.** Ruth voluntarily remains with Naomi and does not remarry, unlike her sister-in-law Orpah. Ruth abides by Naomi's plan to determine Boaz's willingness to perform a pseudo-Levirate marriage. In Ruth's willingness to self-sacrifice her own future, she also forfeited her

Moabite status. Boaz recognized Ruth's unexpected kindness–one that does not expect a reciprocal reward. **This type of kindness is called a *chesed shel emet*.**[20] As a result, Boaz presents Ruth with a new Jewish status by acknowledging her as an *A'shet Chai'yil*.

Ruth's new identity resulted from her kindness to Boaz—shown through her willingness to marry Boaz according to Naomi's plan.

Although Ruth's status changed that night on the threshing floor (Ruth 3:7–14), **the full acceptance of her new status would only happen later**. Remember, Ruth is David's great grandmother and is therefore an ancestor of the messiah. The second rare phrase in verse 3:11 confirms my statement: "all the gate of my nation" (*kol sha'ar ami*) will know you are an *A'shet Chai'yil*. The *kol sha'ar ami* is Boaz's prophetic revelation. The *A'shet Chai'yil* is his declaration that Ruth's new status began the night on the threshing floor. Ruth's future is with God's people. **The *A'shet Chai'yil* declarations that we sing on *Shabbat* remind us that God gives a new identity to anyone who decides to seek Him whole-heartedly.**

---

[20]Carrying the name of the deceased or one involved in the burial of a deceased person is considered a *chesed shel emet* because the deceased individual can never repay the person performing the act. An example of a *chesed shel emet* appears in Genesis 47:29, when Jacob requests Joseph to bury him in Israel and not in Egypt, "And when the time approached for Israel to die, he called his son Joseph and said to him, 'If I have find favor in your eyes, place your hand on my thigh and you will do *chesed emet* (lovingkindness, truth); do not bury me in Egypt'" (Author's translation).

The Blessing of the Children

For years, I have been privileged to host numerous pastors and Christian leaders at my Friday evening *Shabbat* table. **When I laid my hands on my children** and invoked a snippet from Genesis 48:20–"May *Elohim* make you like Ephraim and Manasseh"–and the Priestly Blessing, "May God show you favor and be gracious to you" (Numbers 6:24–26), **tears filled my guests' eyes**. With curiosity I have asked, "Friends, why the tears and the emotions? Have I upset you?" Several responded and humbly admitted, **we "never received a blessing from our parents."** Naturally, I was surprised. In fact, long before I composed the final chapter of *Your Sabbath Invitation*, many Christian friends have been touched by my abridged *verbal* descriptions of the Blessing of the Children.

In Hebrew, the Blessing of the Children is known as *Birkat Habonim*. The *Birkat Habonim* was adopted quite late in the history of Judaism; the earliest records only extend back to the late fourteenth century in Germany.[21] However, do not presume that parents did not bless their offspring prior to the fourteenth century! **In fact, as early as the fifth century, the Genesis 48:20 Ephraim and**

[21]The *Aruch HaShulcan* edited by Rabbi Yechiel Michel Epstein (1829-1908) cites the Rabbi Jacob Halevi Moelin (1360-1427), also called the Maharil, that "he would not bless his children on Friday night when he was in a state of mourning" (ערוך השולחן יורה דעה סימן ת, *Aruch HaShulchan, Yorah De'ah, Siman Taf*). One can deduce that if Rabbi Moelin was not in a state of mourning, then he would certainly bless his children. Rabbi Moelin was born in Mainz, Germany and eventually became the rabbi of the city.

Manasseh blessing was invoked during the circumcision ceremony.[22] Basically, the formal *Birkat Habonim* (Blessing the Children), which incorporates both "May *Elohim* make you like Ephraim and Manasseh" (Genesis 48:20) and the Priestly Blessing (Numbers 6:24–27), originated in the Middle Ages.

As a Jewish father, I derive a special joy from the *Birkat Habonim.* This moving *Shabbat minhag* enables me to **instruct**, **bless**, and **bond face-to-face** with my sons each week! Tangible opportunities to **fortify relationships** with my children are priceless rarities in today's virtual, digital world. Right here, let me reiterate what I said earlier concerning the *minhag A'shet Chai'yil.* **If you are witnessing the Blessing of the Children at a Sabbath celebration, and you are not a father, mother, child, son, or daughter, stay where you are! Do not exit secretly or develop a lukewarm heart.** We Orthodox Jews delight in gatherings and ceremonies that glorify God and upbuild biblical families, whether the family is ours or someone else's. משפחות (*Mish'pa'chot*, families) are important! Furthermore, Psalm 2:11 (Author's translation) declares:

The Blessing of the Children enables you to instruct, bless, bond face-to-face with, and fortify relationships with your children.

[22]See the Jerusalem Targum on Genesis 48:20. The Jerusalem Targum is also known as Targum Jerusalem, Pseudo-Jonathan Targum, or Targum Pseudo-Jonathan.

עִבְדוּ אֶת־יְהוָה בְּיִרְאָה וְגִילוּ בִּרְעָדָה

(*Av'du et Adonai b'yir'at v'gilu bir'a'dah*)

"Serve The Eternal in awe and
rejoice with trembling."[23]

Witnessing the *Birkat Habonim* with a grateful heart is another opportunity to serve God.

Before we unpack the nuances of *Birkat Habonim*, let me remind you that **this particular *Shabbat* blessing is a true *minhag*. The procedures for the *Birkat Habonim* are not outlined in the Torah**–not in the same manner that God explains the offerings in the Book of Leviticus. Nevertheless, the custom is rooted in the Scriptures. The first portion of the *Birkat Habonim* is found in Genesis 48:20. The verse appears in Table 30 (Author's translation):[24]

Table 30. The First Blessing of *Birkat Habonim* (Genesis 48:20)

יְשִׂמְךָ אֱלֹהִים כְּאֶפְרַיִם וְכִמְנַשֶּׁה
Y'sim'cha Elohim k'Efraim v'chi'Menashe
May *Elohim* make you like Ephraim and like Menashe

[23]Both imperative verbs have plural "you" subjects. The Apostle Paul even charged the believers to, "Rejoice with ones who rejoice and weep with ones who weep" (Romans 12:15, Author's translation). *Shabbat* should be an assembly of grateful hearts.

[24]Genesis 48:20 is not the only Scripture that depicts a father bestowing a blessing on his own children (see Genesis 27:27–30).

When I bless my children on *Shabbat*, I do so as their *father*; yet, in Genesis 48:20, a *grandfather* is administering the blessing to *grandchildren who become his children* because Manasseh and Ephraim were Joseph's sons, not Jacob's. So, why was Genesis 48:20 chosen as a foundational text? Is there something unique concerning Manasseh and Ephraim? Furthermore, why do we only recite these four Hebrew words from Genesis 48:20: יְשִׂמְךָ אֱלֹהִים כְּאֶפְרַיִם וְכִמְנַשֶּׁה (*Y'sim'cha Elohim k'Efraim v'chi'Menashe*, May *Elohim* make you like *Ephraim* and like *Menashe*). The truth is, Genesis 48:20 is a rich text. **To appreciate the Blessing of the Children, I suggest that you review Genesis 48 before reading any further.** Please keep your Bibles nearby because the verses are not included here. Instead, I will provide an accurate summary and steer you through some of the nuances and inferences from the text. **This is the last site I will cover as your tour guide.**

Genesis 48:1: Someone told Joseph that his father is חֹלֶה (*choleh*, weak, sick). Joseph goes at once with his two sons, Ephraim and Manasseh.

Points to Ponder: Who is the anonymous person who told Joseph that Jacob is ill? Why did Joseph take Ephraim and Manasseh with him as opposed to going alone?

Genesis 48:2: Someone tells Jacob that Joseph has arrived, but Manasseh and Ephraim are not mentioned. Israel strengthens himself and sits on the bed.

Points to Ponder: Again, we have an anonymous person entering the scene and the individual now informs Jacob of Joseph's arrival. Who is this person? Is this the same individual who told Joseph of Jacob's illness? Should we assume that Manasseh and Ephraim are in the room with Jacob and Joseph or are they waiting outside? From whatever ailment Jacob is suffering, he is able to lift himself from a horizontal position and sit on the bed.

Genesis 48:3–4: Jacob recounts a particular episode in his life when God gave him: 1) the blessings in Luz, which included making him into ***k'hal amim*** (קְהַל עַמִּים, usually translated as "assembly of tribes,"[25] "community of peoples,"[26] "multitude of peoples,"[27] or "multitude of nations"), and 2) the land of Canaan.

Points to Ponder: Jacob is alluding to the *Bet El* event in Genesis 35:6–15, where God: 1) changes his name to Israel; 2) promises him an abundance of progeny, that is a ***k'hal goyim*** (קְהַל גּוֹיִם, generally translated as a "company of nations"); 3) prophesies kings from his loins 4) as well as the land of Canaan. However, **Jacob slightly alters God's promise in Genesis 35:11 from a *k'hal goyim* to a *k'hal amim* and omits the kings' component of the blessing**. Is there a difference between the Hebrew terms *goyim* and *amim*? Why does Jacob omit the kings' blessing, number "3)" in the list?

Genesis 48:5–6: Jacob deems Ephraim and Manasseh as his own children, and any additional children from Joseph

---

[25]E. A. Speiser, *Genesis: Introduction, Translation, and Notes*, Anchor Bible, vol. 1 (New Haven: Yale University Press, 2008), 357.

[26]K. A. Mathews, *New International Version Genesis 11:27–50:26*, The New American Commentary, An Exegetical and Theological Exposition of Holy Scripture, vol. 1B (Nashville: Broadman & Holman Publishers, 2005), 871.

[27]G. J. Wenham, *Genesis 16–50*, Word Biblical Commentary, vol. 2 (Dallas: Word, Incorporated, 1994), 458.

will be recognized as Joseph's offspring with respect to the inheritance laws.

Points to Ponder: Jacob is mentioning Ephraim and Manasseh, so we may assume that he is aware of their presence. **Jacob inconceivably transforms the biological status of Ephraim and Manasseh from grandchildren to children and equates them with his first and second sons, Reuben and Simeon.** Furthermore, Jacob reverses his grandchildren's birth order. **When Jacob matched Ephraim to Reuben and Manasseh to Simeon, he reversed the birth order.** Manasseh is Joseph's firstborn son, not Ephraim.

Genesis 48:7: Jacob recounts Rachel's death and burial on the way to Bethlehem.

Points to Ponder: In the midst of biological transformations and the bequeathing of tribal status to Ephraim and Manasseh, why does Jacob digress to discuss the burial of Rachel?

Addressing all of the curiosities in Genesis 48:1–7 exceeds the scope of *Your Sabbath Invitation.* Nevertheless, we can extract a handful of assumptions from the text:

1. Jacob's illness is serious enough for Joseph, **the most powerful person in Egypt**, to cancel his obligations and go immediately to Goshen to visit his father.
2. Joseph's taking of Manasseh and Ephraim to Goshen exceeds his need for extra family support during Jacob's health crisis. Furthermore, Joseph's sons accompany

> him because they are not toddlers. Oh, I just heard several gasps! "David, I thought Manasseh and Ephraim were small boys?" A hasty reading of Genesis 48:12–13 may imply that Joseph's sons were small, but a careful study of several verses (Genesis 41:46–50; 46:20; 47:9, 28, 29; 48:1; 50:22) confirms that they are young men, likely in their early twenties.

According to the *Midrash Lekach Tov*, the anonymous people in Genesis 48:1–2 could be Manasseh or Ephraim.[30] The *Lekach Tov* is perceptive; It states that Joseph probably asked Manasseh and Ephraim, occasionally, to visit their grandfather or rotate his care with their uncles, Joseph's brothers. **Therefore, I conclude that the Genesis text infers that Jacob told Manasseh and Ephraim that his illness was life-threatening, and that his intentions were to bless them, Joseph, and their uncles.** The only conundrum with my inference is the conversation between Jacob and Joseph in Genesis 48:8–9:

Israel (Jacob): "Who are these?" (Genesis 48:8).

Joseph: "They are my sons, whom *Elohim* gave me in this" (Genesis 48:9).

Israel (Jacob): "Please bring them to me so I can bless them" (Genesis 48:9).

---

[30]*Midrash Lekach Tov*, see *Sefaria.org*, n.p., https://www.sefaria.org/Midrash_Lekach_Tov%2C_Genesis.48.1.4?lang=en&with=all&lang2=en&p3=Genesis.48.6&lang3=en&aliyot3=0/ (9 September 2021).

Why did Jacob (Israel) say, "Who are these?", as if he could not recognize his own grandchildren? We already surmised that Manasseh and Ephraim were both in the room, and according to the *midrash*, one of them informed Jacob that Joseph had arrived. If the only sensible answer involved the grandfather's poor eyesight, then the dialogue between Jacob and Joseph in the *David Nekrutman Version* (my last attempt to edit the Bible) would read as follows:

Israel: [He is unable to recognize his grandchildren because of poor eyesight.] "Who are these?"

Joseph: "Manasseh and Ephraim."

Israel: "Sorry, my eyesight is not as it used to be." [Jacob begins to bless Manasseh and Ephraim.]

This is our **final stop** in *Your Sabbath Invitation.* You know the terrain. What is our strategy for decoding enigmas? We go to the site and excavate for revelation. We review the Jewish hermeneutics. We remember that *midrash* often answers the questions we should have asked. Therefore, we must *analyze* and *question* Israel's (Jacob's) question. Is "Who are these?" **related** or **unrelated to Israel's poor eyesight mentioned in Genesis 48:10? Here is one clue,** the answer lies elsewhere in Genesis 48.

Look again at Genesis 48:3–4 when Jacob first speaks to Joseph. In the "Points to Ponder" section I mentioned two Hebrew phrases, ***k'hal goyim*** (Genesis 35:11) and ***k'hal amim*** (Genesis 48:4). Let's review Genesis 48:3–4:

To understand Jacob's declaration "Who are these," we must decipher the difference between ***k'hal goyim*** and ***k'hal***

amim. Genesis 48:3–4 says, "And Jacob said to Joseph, '*El Shaddai* appeared to me in Luz, in the land of Canaan and He blessed me. And He said to me, "Behold I will make you fruitful and cause you to multiply, and I will make you into a ***k'hal amim*** (קְהַל עַמִּים), and I will give you this land, and your offspring, for an everlasting possession"""(Author's translation).

The translations for ***k'hal amim*** vary from "assembly of tribes," "community of peoples," "multitude of peoples," or "multitude of nations." In Genesis 48, through Ephraim and Manasseh, Jacob is trying to manifest what God promised him in Genesis 35:9-12 decades earlier! **Pay attention because this final nugget is incredible.** (All of God's nuggets are incredible!)

> *Elohim* appeared to Jacob once again when he came to Padan Aram and blessed him. *Elohim* said to him, "Your name Jacob, you will no longer be called by the name of Jacob anymore because your name is Israel, and He called his name Israel." And *Elohim* said to him, "I, *El Shaddai*, be fruitful and multiply, *goy* and ***k'hal goyim*** will come from you, and kings will come from your loins. And the land I gave to Abraham and to Isaac, I will give you and your offspring will I give the land" (Author's translation).

In one instant God changes Jacob's name to Israel and transforms his identity. God also promised Jacob

(Israel) progeny, *goy*, *k'hal goyim*, and kings, **but the only challenge to the prophecy was that Jacob would not be having any more children.** His twelve males and one female (Dinah) were already born and grown. As Jacob's days begin to end, **Jacob enacts an ancestral *identity change* through his grandchildren Ephraim and Manasseh**. He declares to his son Joseph, "And now, your two sons, who were born to you in the land of Egypt, until I came to you, to the land of Egypt they are [literally] mine. Ephraim and Manasseh will be like Reuben and Simeon to me. Your progeny after their birth will be yours…" (Genesis 48:5–6, Author's translation). When Jacob says, "Who are these," **he is making a final declaration that Ephraim and Manasseh's familial identity would now be as *his own* children, not as his grandsons.** When Joseph responds, "They [Ephraim and Manasseh] are my sons, whom *Elohim* gave me in this," this was the last time Joseph could claim that these two sons were entirely his. **Now Ephraim and Manasseh gained recognition as distinct tribes within the nation of Israel.**

God changed Jacob's name to Israel and promised him descendants—but Jacob would not have any more children!

Ephraim and Manasseh would now be identified as Jacob's sons, not as his grandchildren.

Changing the ancestral identity is not a trivial, inconsequential act. Tribal identity was completely related to land and inheritance issues. When the twelve tribes entered Canaan, Ephraim and Manasseh would receive allotments in conjunction with Jacob's other sons. Joseph is indeed one of Jacob's twelve sons, but now his identity is fused within Ephraim and Manasseh. **What is truly amazing about the identity change is that Ephraim and Manasseh are children from an intermarriage!** Their father Joseph is from Jacob, but their mother, Asenath, is the daughter of an Egyptian priest. Do not forget that Egyptians descend from Ham, the son of Noah (Genesis 10:6). The values of the Egyptian civilization were contrary to the God of Abraham, Isaac, and Jacob. Despite the Egyptian heritage of his grandsons, Jacob still promotes Ephraim and Manasseh to the level of Reuben and Simeon. **How does Jacob have the license to take children reared in the Egyptian pagan culture to become tribes of Israel**?

Readers, this is exactly the point: **Ephraim and Manasseh did not identify as Egyptians! They identified themselves as Israelites.** The idea that Ephraim and Manasseh are Israelites is also derived from Genesis 41:50, "Two sons were born to Joseph before the year of the famine, whom Asenath daughter of Potiphera **bore to him**." Why does the verse emphasize that the children were born to Joseph instead of simply saying "Joseph and Asenath had Ephraim and Manasseh"? **The statement indicates that Asenath followed the God of Abraham, Isaac, and**

> *Asenath followed her husband Joseph's God and did not rear her children according to Egypt's pagan culture.*

Jacob, and **she did not rear the children in accordance with the Egyptian pagan culture**.

When Joseph says, "They are my sons, whom *Elohim* gave me in this," **he understands that as a result of Ephraim and Manasseh maintaining their faith in God, they can become a federation of tribes under the sovereignty of God that Jacob wishes to manifest.**

When we are blessing our children on Friday evening with the snippet from Genesis 48:20, we are cognizant of the substantial context behind the verse. **The Divine gift that Ephraim and Manasseh received for maintaining their faith in the God of Israel came through their grandfather Jacob (Israel) and resulted in an historic identity change.** Ephraim and Manasseh were elevated from their respectable positions as *individual heirs under the tribe of Joseph* to full entitlement, authority, inheritance, and privilege *as a tribe of Israel.* The blessing of Ephraim and Manasseh testifies that our children will be reared to awe the God of Abraham, Isaac, and Jacob.

Conclusion

Halleluyah! *Your Sabbath Invitation* readers, I am thrilled! **Not only do you have practical tools to conduct *Shabbat* in your own homes, but you also have a respectable biblical and historical foundation to accompany your celebration.** Remember, the information in this chapter is designed *especially for Christians*. It is not formulated for Orthodox Jews who follow the Sabbath. In short, I do not recommend that you invite any Jewish neighbors to substitute this primer for their more elaborate customs! Moreover, many Orthodox Jews conduct their *Shabbatot* (plural of *Shabbat*) in Hebrew, **which gives you a great incentive to learn Hebrew**. So, **I am ecstatic if you are willing and able to implement *any* of my recommendations.**

> *Conducting Shabbat in your own home is a great incentive to learn Hebrew.*

One of the primary figurative conceptual characters in the final chapter of *Your Sabbath Invitation* is "**identity**." **Ruth** received a brand-new identity when Boaz prophetically called her *A'shet Chai'yil*. **Ephraim and Manasseh** obtained new, unexpected birthright identities comparable to Israel's twelve beloved sons. **Identity significantly changed the lives of these three biblical figures.**

Another important character is "**redemption**." While I did not discuss redemption heavily, the subject is essential in the Book of Ruth. **Ruth not only obtained a new identity, but she was also *redeemed*.** Her future was bleak and penniless. Boaz was her kinsman redeemer. Ruth's story reminds us that the Torah offers supreme redemption. Similarly, Adam was not only redeemed from a hopeless future, he was also spared from death on *Shabbat*. *Shabbat* was the attorney who defended Adam from instantaneous death.

When we sing the *A'shet Chai'yil*, we experience redemption anew. When we recite Psalm 92 on the Sabbath, we are reminded of what the Sabbath means to humanity. **During *Shabbat* we experience the Amplified Presence of God manifested in the *Shekinah*. The Sabbath is an**

opportunity for all of humanity to experience God and to discover or deepen their identity in Him. *Shabbat* reminds us that redemption is available to all who sincerely desire to seek God.

> *Shabbat is an opportunity for humanity to discover or deepen their* ***identity*** *in God, and a reminder that* ***redemption*** *is available to all who seek God!*

Notes

Your Sabbath Invitation

Epilogue

Congratulations! You finished your journey through *Your Sabbath Invitation*! You did it! I realize that some chapters required serious hiking while others felt like a boat ride on the calm waters of the Sea of Galilee during the spring season. I sincerely hope that each chapter provided you with spiritual nuggets to deepen your relationship with God; and I hope you viewed the *Shabbat* invitation as an opportunity to soak in His Amplified Presence. Today, you understand the value of Biblical Hebrew because English translations have limitations. In retrospect, you fully appreciate the practice of mining Scripture and decoding Hebrew words like an expert. So, excavating revelation has become a mode for experiencing incredible God-soul moments, rather than another occasion for taxing academic work.

To be upfront and personal, I dreaded writing this Epilogue! How does an author say goodbye to his readers? From this point forward, we share an author-reader connection through the words in this book. Furthermore, to my delight, I am also a pipeline, although not as monumental as our ancestor Adam! God has placed a desire in my heart to serve as a conduit that supports the fulfillment of Isaiah 66:23 in some small manner. I still marvel because the entry into my "new calling" began on the back of an Israeli tour bus at the end of 2019, where seeds were planted to write *Your Sabbath Invitation*. The book required considerable prayers and intense reflection to compose; regular presentations to a core group of people; and working intimately–almost daily–with my editors Pam and Samir Idriss.

I stated in the introduction that I would be the *moreh* (teacher) and you would act as *talmidim* (students), but the model is slightly flawed. In Jewish learning, the *moreh-talmidim* relationship is dynamic and familial, and unfortunately, I do not have any personal interactions with most of you–my cherished readers. I am unacquainted with your family histories or your dreams and aspirations. I know nothing about the struggles and hardships you have faced in life. The same is true for you–how well do you really know me? Let me adjust the inadequate paradigm right now.

Frankly speaking, I have not always fulfilled the *Shabbat* revelations outlined in this book. Yes, I am guilty of treating *Shabbat* as a routine! "Impossible! Did David Nekrutman really do that?" There were times I longed for *Shabbat* to end early because I wanted to enjoy certain leisurely activities or complete work on a deadline. In other seasons of my life, I viewed *Shabbat* as an opportunity to recapture needed sleep after an exhausting workweek. I confess that a fear of heavenly consequences often served as the deterrent for not violating *Shabbat*. In the balance between the proper intention to fulfill God's mandates and the actual execution of the Divine directives, I have often committed to the routine of the practice while excluding a passionate and attentive heart.

What I am saying is that I am a flawed human being. During my mediocre moments, the Christians who have eaten at my *Shabbat* table have unknowingly reminded me, time and time again, about the gift of *Shabbat*. It is ironic to me that my engagement with Christians has made me a better Jew. God has planted people in my life to help me appreciate features within my spiritual life as a committed Jew that I am prone to undervalue.

Writing *Your Sabbath Invitation* in the last twenty months has moved me to apologize to God for not properly stewarding *Shabbat*. During this demanding period, I have developed and integrated a greater anticipation for the Sabbath. Most importantly, I have discovered that *Shabbat* is not an elite club for celebrities. The Sabbath is open for all of humanity who believe in the God of Abraham, Isaac, and Jacob. Isaiah witnessed a sliver of fulfilled prophecy in his lifetime, and he envisioned and prophesied that one day all of humanity [who believe] will celebrate *Shabbat*.

There is a story of a young rabbi who desired to change the world. Soon he realized that his aspiration was quite difficult to achieve. So, the rabbi modified his vision to a simpler endeavor–one of helping his community of faith draw closer to God. Eventually, he also found his reduced vision too challenging to accomplish. Finally, the rabbi focused his efforts on his family, but some of his children did not follow his path. When he became an elderly person, he had an epiphany that if he had diligently worked on his own character traits, then he would have impacted his family and generated a tide of ripple effects that could have influenced his community of faith and perhaps the entire world.

Although I have called myself a "teacher," it is you, the readers, who have taught me. *Your Sabbath Invitation* marks a new calling in my life–a calling that involves more teaching and writing about *Shabbat*. Recently, I have rediscovered precepts about *Shabbat* that have irrevocably touched a chord in my soul. After presenting the material in this book to Bible study groups and churches around the world, I have become a better Bible educator. Throughout my *Your Sabbath Invitation* journey, I have worked fervently on myself so that I can become a better and more committed person to God.

I thank you, dear reader, for an opportunity to pen the words for *Your Sabbath Invitation*. In some measure, we have moved closer to becoming one with each other. What do I mean? God breathed His breath into the soul of the first human being. We are all the results of God's exhaled breath. Our individual souls come from One Source. God created the *Shabbat* for us to witness in the world that He alone is the Creator of all. He is the ultimate authority for everything in this world and His Presence permeates every aspect of our lives. Before us is a unique opportunity where we can become one–by accepting God's original invitation. Let us join together "soul-to-soul" and partner with Him in the ultimate celebration as witnesses to the world that He alone is God.

Glossary

Detailed Explanations of Select Words and Phrases

---

appointed times

Within the context of the Bible, the special days God sets aside to commune with humanity or the Jewish people. Appointed times (*mo'a'dim*) are not optional. Committed Jewish people are required to observe appointed times. Leviticus 23 lists the appointed times, which some describe as "holidays" or "feasts," although "times" is the most accurate term. The *mo'a'dim* that occur in the spring season include: Passover (*Pesach*) and Festival of Weeks (*Shavuot*). The Fall *mo'a'dim* include the Jewish New Year (*Rosh HaShanah*), Day of Atonement (*Yom Kippur*), Feast of Tabernacles (*Sukkot*), and Eighth Day (*Shmini Azeret*).

Author's translation

The phrase indicates that an author translated a literary work from one language (the "source" or "original" language) into another language (the "target" or "receptor" language). In the academic study of Scripture, "Author's translation" usually applies to scholars who develop their own translations of biblical texts from ancient manuscripts and documents. The term presumes an expertise in biblical languages. At the ORU Graduate School of Theology and Ministry, those of us who had obtained proficiency in biblical or ancient languages such as, Biblical Hebrew, Biblical Greek, Aramaic, Syriac, or others, were required to translate large portions of Scripture in our Master of Arts theses, then cite our results with "Author's translation." In addition, my years in an Orthodox *yeshiva* and my fluency in Biblical Hebrew and Modern Hebrew *humbly* qualify me to use "Author's translation" in *Your Sabbath Invitation.* A *yeshiva* is the Jewish educational system available to students beyond the elementary school level. College-aged and post-graduate students can also attend *yeshivot* (plural of *yeshiva*). *Yeshiva* students meticulously study and discuss the Torah, the Talmud, numerous rabbinic texts, and Jewish *Halakhah* (law). Currently, Israel and the United States have the highest number of *yeshivot.*

Several categories of Bible translations exist including, "word-for-word," "literal," "paraphrased," "dynamic," and "functional equivalence." A discussion of these particular types exceeds *Your Sabbath Invitation.*

autonomic nervous system

The portion of the nervous system that automatically controls actions and tasks in the human body, without deliberate or voluntary input from an individual. Some of the tasks include breathing, digestion, elimination, and monitoring and regulating the body's temperature, blood pressure, and fluid levels.

Babylonian Talmud

After the Hebrew Bible, the Talmud is the most important assemblage of religious writings in Judaism. The Talmud consists of two main sections–the Mishnah and the Gemarah. The Mishnah is a compendium of Jewish law canonized around 200 CE, and the Gemarah is the authoritative rabbinic commentary on the Mishnah. The Talmud is almost unlimited in content because it addresses hundreds of topics in philosophy, biology, and psychology. The Talmud is also a storehouse of legends, proverbs, and wisdom, encompassing the work of Jewish sages who lived in the land of Israel and in Babylon, from the end of the Second Temple Period (516 BCE–70 CE) through the start of the Middle Ages. The Babylonian Talmud consists of sixty-three tractates. A tractate is written material that concentrates on a particular subject. For example, Tractate *Shabbat* provides law and commentary about *Shabbat*. The Talmud embodies the concepts of study and wisdom through masterful teachings on: 1) the positive religious duty of studying Torah; 2) the virtue of acquiring wisdom; and 3) the inherent reward of study alone. (The definition of the Talmud is adapted from Adin Steinsaltz, *The Essential Talmud*, 30th ed. [New York: Basic Books, 2006].)

dra'sh

The three-letter Hebrew root is "דרש," which means "seek." *Dra'sh* is a familiar verb that appears throughout the Hebrew Bible. When applied specifically to Bible study, to "*dra'sh*" involves seeking God by exploring every facet of a Scripture. The word is frequently affiliated with *midrash*. The title of chapter 8 is ***Dra'shing***, where *Your Sabbath Invitation* introduced *midrash* for the first time. *Dra'shing* is an English vernacular for practicing *dra'sh*.

end of time

For many Orthodox Jews and specifically in *Your Sabbath Invitation*, the term signifies the inauguration of the Messianic Age. Most Orthodox Jewish Zionists believe that the Messianic Age started with the advent of the State of Israel. In *Your Sabbath Invitation*, the "Messianic Age" and the "end of time" represent the same period. Characteristics of the Messianic Age include health, economic prosperity, and peace between nations. For many Christians, the end of time began after Jesus' birth and will continue until His promised Second Coming. Acts 1 and 2 also speak of the last days.

etymology

The study of a word's (or words') origin, derivation, and multiple forms throughout the word's (words') linguistic history. Ordinarily, the process reveals various meanings the word or words have possessed over time. Sometimes, in order to determine or clarify a word's meaning, the *smallest division of a word*–known as a *morpheme*–is examined and compared to a word in another language that is linguistically similar.

exegesis

An investigation of a word or text to ascertain its meaning in the original context, environment, and setting. Initially, exegesis applied to religious texts, but the term is used for other literary genres today. Exegesis originated from the Greek word ἐξήγησις (*exegesis*). A *simple* exegesis may involve a Bible dictionary, commentary, or a concordance. A concordance alphabetically locates key words from a particular book or text. Some Bible concordances include a Hebrew and Greek lexicon (dictionary) that identifies the original Hebrew and Greek roots for each word. When scholars conduct a *critical* exegesis, they perform an extensive investigation and analysis of a word's original language, linguistics, grammar, ancient cultural basis and more. To summarize, an exegesis "reads out" the meaning of a word or text–objectively–while an "eisegesis" "reads" an individual's own interpretation "into" the word or text. Seek exegesis!

Heavenly Torah

The **infinite**, intangible word of God that has always existed. The term "Heavenly" identifies what is Divine and Eternal. The tangible written Torah, which we read and study on earth, is **finite**. Here, the word "Torah" applies to the entire Hebrew Bible not only to the five Books of Moses. Humanity transcribed the Heavenly Torah–God's Eternal words–through Divine inspiration. Qualified biblical figures (Abraham, Rebekah, and Joseph) were able to access the Heavenly Torah via the Holy Spirit. Accessing the Heavenly Torah intensifies one's relationship with God. God also used the Heavenly Torah to create the world.

lived experience of the *Shekinah*

The action of the *Shekinah* (please read the definition of "The *Shekinah*" first), which moved an individual, family, or community to create a *minhag.* A "lived experience of the *Shekinah*" is not restricted to *minhagim* (plural of *minhag*). One can encounter a lived experience of the *Shekinah* by engaging in the study of Torah.

midrash, midrashim, Midrash, Midrashim

Read the comprehensive explanation in Appendix A-1, "The Essentials of *midrash* and *Midrash.*"

minhag

The basic English translation is "custom," although the term concerns much more. The *minhagim* (plural of *minhag*) emerged from a move of God within the family and/or community to demonstrate their fidelity to God. The three-letter root is "נהג" (*nahag*) which means "to lead." The Hebrew word "מנהג" (*minhag*) appears in 2 Kings 9:20. There, מנהג means "driving" and refers to the driving of Jehu's chariot. *Minhagim* incorporate a large range of practices that express the individual's or community's religious lifestyles.

nikud, nikudot

The *nikudot* (singular is *nikud*) are Hebrew vowels. They are part of the ancient vocalization (pronunciation) system designed to accompany the Hebrew consonants. The *nikudot* are the small dots and dashes that rest below, above, or in the center of a Hebrew consonant. *Nikudot* occur in most Hebrew Bibles and throughout *Your Sabbath Invitation*. For centuries, the Hebrew Scriptures were passed down through oral transmission. During the Middle ages, a family of Tiberian scribes, the *Masoretes*, adapted written *nikudot* to the Scriptures in order to preserve and guard the vocalizations. The *nikudot* represent five sounds, which echo the English sounds: AH, EH, EE, OH, and OO. The vowel *shva* has no sound. Below is an illustration of the primary *nikudot* applied to the Hebrew letters *hey* (ה), *lamed* (ל), *aleph* (א), *vav* (ו), and *gimel* (ג):

גֶ גֻ גַ גָ גֵ גִ גְ וֹ וּ אֱ אֳ אֲ לַי הֵי

For a pronunciation guide of the *nikudot*, see **Hebrew Translations and English Pronunciations** in the section below entitled "Hebrew Words."

The *Shekinah*

The *Shekinah* is the feminine aspect of God and a manifestation of the Holy Spirit. *Midrashically, A'shet Chai'yil* is the pronoun which represents the *Shekinah* and the Torah. The *Shekinah* refers to the modified (*Ruach Hakodesh*) Holy Spirit. In Judaism, the full Embodiment of the *Ruach Hakodesh* was removed from our earthly realm sometime in the early part of the Second Temple Period (516 BCE–70 CE). With the advent of the State of Israel and the ingathering of the Jewish People from the four corners of the world, many Orthodox Jews believe that we are living in a period where some of the aspects of the Holy Spirit are revealed.

Torah

The Hebrew word for Torah is תורה (*to'rah*). An excellent translation (definition) of Torah is "instructions." The word Torah can represent: (1) the Pentateuch–Five Books of Moses; (2) a general term for all of God's instructions, requirements, laws, and commandments; (3) the entire written and canonized Hebrew Bible; or 4) specific passages or verses. Metaphorically, the Torah is God's soul. The Torah is also viewed as the real operating system of the world. On earth we read a finite written Torah that is connected to the infinite Heavenly Torah. Moses received the written Torah 3500 years ago at Sinai. The Torah is multifaceted. Thus, the context determines the applicable definition for the Torah.

Torah Scroll

A Torah Scroll contains the five Books of Moses–Genesis (**בְּרֵאשִׁית**, *B'rei'shit*, At the Beginning), Exodus (**שְׁמוֹת**, *Sh'mote*, Names), Leviticus (**וַיִּקְרָא**, *Va'yiq'ra*, And He Called), Numbers (**בְּמִדְבַּר**, *B'mid'bar*, In the Desert), and Deuteronomy (**דְּבָרִים**, *D'va'reem*, Words). The Torah Scroll is תורה (*To'rah*). Torah Scrolls **must be** written by a *sofer*, a highly skilled, pious scribe and composed on kosher parchments using a special ink. Torah Scrolls lack *nikudot*, but they do contain *parshiyot* (units of texts). Torah Scrolls are cherished and normally embellished with vestments and a crown. On Mondays, Thursdays, and *Shabbat*, as well as holidays and fast days, a designated set of Scriptures must be read publicly from a Torah Scroll. If a Torah Scroll becomes invalid through damage, the Scroll must be buried.

transcription, translation, transliteration

In linguistics and speech, the four terms are extremely technical and easy to confuse. Transliteration and transcription methods vary from language to language and from book to book, but specialized, international formats exist in many disciplines (academics, linguistics, religion, science, and more). The easiest way to distinguish and understand the terms is according to their *intended, primary* goals.

transcription–The process of writing (by hand or electronically) a **pronunciation** of a foreign word using an alphabet from another language. A transcription is also the word that results. Ordinarily, the "another language" involves the individual's native tongue and native alphabet. Technically, the transcriptions in *Your Sabbath Invitation* may be categorized as *foreign language transcriptions*. **Pronunciation** is the *primary* goal of a transcription.

translation–The process of writing or expressing the **meaning** of a foreign word in another language. A translation also signifies the words and text that result. **Understanding** is the *primary* goal of a translation, not representation or pronunciation.

transliteration–The process of **converting** or writing (by hand or electronically) a foreign word from one language into a second language using the alphabet of the second language. "Transliteration" refers to the process and to the converted word. Most of the time, transliterations yield excellent pronunciations, but their *primary* goal is to **represent foreign words** in another alphabet, not to pronounce them.

In parentheses, throughout *Your Sabbath Invitation*, I provide convenient, "user-friendly" transliterations and transcriptions **designed to help you recognize, read, and pronounce foreign terms**. Basically, most of my provisions are a combination of a transliteration and a transcription. Below is an example of how **שבת** appears as a **transliteration** and as a **transcription**, where both utilize an international format. Also shown is the combined format that I apply in *Your Sabbath Invitation.*

שַׁבָּת

This is the **original Hebrew word** with the Hebrew vowels or *nikudot* (see the *nikudot* entry above).

–International Format–

šabāt

This is a **transliteration**, a conversion of the Hebrew letters from שַׁבָּת into English. The transliteration uses the English alphabet and special international symbols. Thus, the *ša*=שַׁ; the *bā*=בָּ; and the *t*=ת. Remember, the *primary* goal is to **represent** the word שַׁבָּת in English.

shab-baht

This is a **transcription**, an English **pronunciation** for שַׁבָּת. The transcription only uses the letters of the English alphabet.

–Format in Your Sabbath Invitation–

Shabbat

This is a combination of a **transliteration** and a **transcription**. The combination is used throughout *Your Sabbath Invitation.*

Notes

HEBREW WORDS

Hebrew Transliterations and English Pronunciations

The Hebrew Alphabet with Transliterations

א	(only vowels)	ז	z	ס	s
בּ	b	ח	ch (as in *Bach*)	ע	(only vowels)
ב	v	ט	t	פּ	p
גּ	g	י	y (or i vowel)	פ, ף	f
ג	g	כּ	k	צ, ץ	tz
דּ	d	כ, ך	kh (same as *ch*)	ק	k
ד	d	ל	l	ר	r
ה	h	מ, ם	m	שׁ	sh
ו	v (or o, u vowels)	נ, ן	n	שׂ	s
				ת, תּ	t

1) א and ע are **never** consonants. Their sounds depend on the vowel.
2) ו is the consonant "v" or the vowels "o" and "u."
3) י is the consonant "y" or the vowel "i."
4) ך, ם, ן, ף, ץ are the "final forms" of כ, מ, נ, פ, צ.
Final forms must appear at the **end** of a word.

The *Nikudot* (Vowels) with Transliterations

—ָ	a	—ֶ	e	—ִ	i	וּ	u
—ַ	a	—ֱ	e	—ֹ	o	—ַי	ai
—ֲ	a	—ְ	e (vocal *sh'va*)	וֹ	o	—ֵי	ei
—ֵ	e	—ִי	i	—ֻ	u		

The "—" represents a Hebrew letter. All of the *nikudot* rest **below the letter** *except* וֹ and וּ. Pronounce the *nikudot* by the English vowel beside it. The pronunciations are close approximations; use the chart on the next page.

Pronunciation of English Vowels and Special Sounds

a	as in	*father*	**ai**	as in	*aisle*
e	as in	*hey* or *get*	**ei**	as in	*reign*
i	as in	*marine* or *bit*	**ch**	as in	*Bach*
o	as in	*throw*	**tz**	as in	*waltz*
u	as in	*mule*			

Dictionary of Hebrew Words

Below is an abridged dictionary of select Hebrew words from *Your Sabbath Invitation.* The entries are alphabetized according to their transliteration or transcription; the Hebrew words appear in parentheses to the right of each transcription and transliteration.

Adom (אָדָם)

the proper noun for the first human being

A'ni (אֲנִי)

the first person singular pronoun "I"

Ano'chi (אָנֹכִי)

a seldom used alternative form of the first person singular pronoun "I" that is found in the Hebrew Bible

a'sa (עָשָׂה)

a verb meaning "he had done"

asher shama Avraham b'koli (אֲשֶׁר־שָׁמַע אַבְרָהָם בְּקֹלִי)

literally, "that Abraham listened to My voice," which means (in Genesis 26:5) Abraham followed explicit orders from God

bara (בָּרָא)

In Genesis 1, *bara* means "He (God) created"; the word conveys "authority."

ba'yom ha'sh'vi'e (בַּיּוֹם הַשְּׁבִיעִי)

"with the seventh day"

b'nei Yisrael (בְּנֵי יִשְׂרָאֵל)

children of Israel

bra'cha (בְּרָכָה)

a noun meaning "blessing"; connotes "more of" in Genesis 2:3

cha'mu'shim (חֲמֻשִׁים)

mercenaries

cha'ta'ti (חָטָאתִי)

"I sinned"

Chavah (חַוָּה)

Adom's wife, the first woman,"Eve"

chu'ko'tai (חֻקּוֹתַי)

In the context of Genesis 26:5, they are Divine directives that lack human reason. God gives the order, and we humbly obey Him and fulfill His will.

dra'sh /dra'shing (דרש)

A verb that means "to seek"; in *Your Sabbath Invitation*, the process of excavating biblical texts; from it comes "*dra'shing*" an English vernacular for practicing *dra'sh*

Elohim (אֱלֹהִים)

Elohim is a proper noun for one of God's names that describes His Attribute of Strict Justice. *Elohim* should be translated as "All Powerful."

erev rav (עֵרֶב רַב)

the mixed multitude that went out of Egypt with the Children of Israel

et (עֵת)

"point in time" or "duration of time"

e'tim (עִתִּים)

the plural form of ***et*** (עֵת); "points in time" or "durations of time"

ha'am (הָעָם)

"the nation"

ka'dosh (קָדוֹשׁ)

The term is commonly translated as "holy," "designated," or "separate." Rabbi Friedman's translation is "transparent."

ke'du'sha (קְדֻשָּׁה)

The term is normally translated as "sanctification." Rabbi Friedman prefers "transparency."

ki'yim (קִיַּם)

"fulfilled"

me'kol m'lach'toe (מִכָּל־מְלַאכְתּוֹ)

"from His work"

midrash (מדרש), ***midrashim*** (מדרשים)

Three short definitions are: 1) the process of seeking biblical revelations from the Scriptures; 2) the biblical revelations themselves; and 3) a creative way to unravel unanswered biblical questions. A *midrash* often answers the questions we should have asked. The plural form of *midrash* is *midrashim.* See Appendix A-1, "The Essentials of *midrash* and *Midrash.*"

Midrash (מדרש), ***Midrashim*** (מדרשים)

As a proper noun, *Midrash* is the authoritative compilation of biblical revelations–a rabbinic, multidimensional commentary on Scripture. The *midrashim* (the plural form of *midrash*) comprise many books, but the work is still viewed as one commentary. See Appendix A-1, "The Essentials of *midrash* and *Midrash.*"

minhag (מנהג)

Basically, a *minhag* is a "custom," a spontaneous move of God from an individual, congregation, or community that expresses devotion and loyalty to Torah; the plural is *minhagim. Minhagim* are often performed on *Shabbat.*

mitz'vo'tai (מִצְוֹתַי)

in the context of Genesis 26:5, Divine directives that are logical and reasonable from a human perspective

miz'mor (מִזְמוֹר)

a sincere, emotionally charged, wordless melody

mo'a'dim (מוֹעֲדִים)

"appointed times"

mo'ed (מוֹעֵד)

"appointed time"

o'neg (עֹנֶג)

in Isaiah 55:2, commonly translated as "delight" or "pleasure;" associated with purchasing, preparing, and enjoying special tasty foods on *Shabbat*

or (אוֹר)

in Genesis 1, always translated as "light" in English Bibles; conceptually, "linear time"

parsha (פַּרְשָׁה), ***parshiyot*** (פַּרְשִׁיּוֹת)

a unit of Hebrew text in the Torah Scroll; *parshiyot* are units of Hebrew text

Ruach Hakodesh (רוּחַ הַקֹּדֶשׁ)

The Holy Spirit

Shekinah (שכינה)

basically, the Amplified Presence of God and the feminine aspect of God

shir (שִׁיר)

A *shir* is a product of contemplation, consideration, and language. The standard translation is "song." Its final form always contains words, rhymes, or poetry.

Shomer Shabbat (שֹׁמֵר שַׁבָּת)

Shabbat Anticipator

Tanakh (תנ"ך)

Hebrew Bible

Torah (תורה)

The preferred definition is "instructions." Torah refers to the Five Books of Moses (the Pentateuch); to the entire written and canonized Hebrew Bible; to God's requirements, laws, and commandments in general; or to specific Scriptures. Context determines which definition applies.

toro'tai (תּוֹרֹתָי)

in the context of Genesis 26:5, learning process moments that God used to instruct Abraham how to internalize His Torah further

va'ye'kadesh (וַיְקַדֵּשׁ)

in the context of Genesis 2:3, "and He made Himself Transparent"

va'ye'va'rech (וַיְבָרֶךְ)

in the context of Genesis 2:3, "and He amplified His presence [so humanity can connect to Him]"

va'yish'boat (וַיִּשְׁבֹּת)

literally, "and he ceased"; in the context of Genesis 2:2, "and He ceased"

va'yishmor mish'mar'ti (וַיִּשְׁמֹר מִשְׁמַרְתִּי)

In the context of Genesis 26:5, Abraham was a *Shabbat* anticipator

z'man (זְמַן)

"a specific span of time"

z'ma'nim (זְמַנִים)

"specific spans of time"

APPENDIX

The Essentials of *midrash* and *Midrash*

Below is an outline of basic definitions and facts concerning the words *midrash* and *Midrash*:

1. **Definition of *midrash***

   a. The **process** of seeking deeper, often clarifying, revelations from the Hebrew Bible according to ancient rabbinic techniques and purposes.

   b. A creative method for *unraveling*, *answering*, or *not answering* specific questions, curiosities, and complexities found in the sacred text. The creativity of *midrash* permits more than one interpretation of a biblical verse but **does not automatically accept every interpretation!**

   c. A creative method for *communicating* and *clarifying* any topic or curiosity found in the sacred text.

d. A **way of pondering or probing** the text of the Hebrew Scriptures.

e. True *midrash* has established creative boundaries.

2. Definition of *Midrash*

Midrash is **the multidimensional commentary** on Scripture. The single word "commentary" is correct, but the authoritative Jewish *midrashim* (the plural of *midrash*) are not housed in one massive book. The *midrashim* are **contained** in over thirty different titles such as, *Pirkei de-Rabbi Eliezer*, *Midrash Jonah*, *Midrash Samuel*, and *Yalkhut Shimoni*. Nevertheless, despite the many functions, colorful intricacies, and diverse subjects found in *midrashim*, we still regard the larger *midrashim* commentary as a unified, centralized source for clarification, elucidation, and instruction.

3. Brief Origins and How *Midrash* Operates

The *Chazal* are viewed as the authors/originators of *midrash*. The word ***Chazal*** is an acronym for the Hebrew phrase **ח**כמינו **ז**כרונם **ל**ברכה (*hakhameinu zikhronam livrakhah*), which means "Our Sages of Blessed Memory" (Author's translation). The most important *midrashim* arise from the *Chazal*. Their *midrashim* appear in the Talmud and a host of other sacred, canonized, revered Jewish books. Originally, *midrashim* were memorized, repeated, passed down orally from generation to generation, then recorded. The earliest *Chazal* devised *midrashim* in the first century

CE because they required straightforward, captivating interpretations as well as convenient methods for teaching complex Scriptures to their students and congregations. **In addition, the *Chazal* viewed *midrash* as a way to achieve a closer relationship with God.** Throughout the centuries, as the teaching needs of the *Chazal* and rabbis changed, the literary features of *midrash* also changed. As a result, later interpretive approaches from other respected rabbis diverged from the *Chazal*. Finally, *midrash* and *midrashic* techniques are considerably different from standard Christian biblical hermeneutics.

4. **Goals of *midrash***–The *Chazal*'s *midrashim* involved the following:

    a. **Significance**: The *Chazal* recognized that every word and vowel marking in Scripture has a **significance** that must be understood, especially words or phrases that seem "redundant." (I address potential redundancies in chapter 12.)

    b. **Missing details**: Although the biblical narratives are thorough, they omit details. So, the *Chazal* devised imaginative *midrashim* to provide any **missing details** and to clarify possible discrepancies in the text.

Reading remote verses: Normally, the *Chazal* read Bible verses within the context of **remote (non-neighboring) verses** and not exclusively within their immediate contexts. Thus, the *Chazal* achieved two results: 1) They vigorously resolved *apparent* contradictions in the sacred text because the Bible cannot contradict itself!;

and 2) They juxtaposed linguistically or thematically similar verses in order to highlight or uncover meanings that exceeded what each verse conveyed alone.

5. Two Types of Midrash

Midrash Halakhah–The word *Halakhah* means "the walk" or "the way we walk." The *Halakhic midrashim* focus on legal matters and decisions related to obeying the laws and ordinances in the Torah. (The word "legal" in Judaism is **not entirely synonymous** with "legal" in American English. Generally, the American usage connotes taking someone to court. The word "legal" in Judaism signifies "related to obeying Torah.") The *Talmud*, *Mishnah*, and the *Mekhilta* (on *Shemot*–Exodus) are three *Halakhic midrashim.*

Midrash Aggadah–The word *Aggadah* means "story, tale, or lesson." Essentially, *Aggadah* is **everything** that is not *Halakhah.* The *Aggadic midrashim* include history, poetry, allegories, stories, parables, and moral instructions, lessons, and sermons. The *Bereishit Rabbah* (*Genesis Rabbah*) and *Midrash Iyyov* (Job) are two *Aggadic midrashim.*

Midrashim often retain characteristics of *Halakhah* and *Aggadah.* So, the *Chazal*'s final *midrash* becomes one tapestry containing multiple, intertwined, interpretive techniques.

Your Sabbath Invitation* contains material from *midrash Halakhah* and *midrash Aggadah.

Adom and *Ha'Adom*

Adom is the transliteration for the Hebrew word אָדָם. The term *Adom* in the Hebrew Bible generally means "humanity" or "man"; however, *Adom* has several meanings in the first five chapters of Genesis.

When God contemplates and creates humanity in Genesis 1:26–27, He uses two terms *Adom* (אָדָם) and *Ha'Adom* (הָאָדָם). Both terms incorporate the maleness (*za'char*) and the femaleness (*n'kay'vah*) that were conjoined together in the first human being. The word אָדָם appears first in Genesis 1:26. Here, אָדָם means **the first human being**:

"וַיֹּאמֶר אֱלֹהִים נַעֲשֶׂה **אָדָם**"

Va'yo'mer Elohim na'a'seh ***Adom***

"And *Elohim* said, 'Let us make ***Adom***'"

(Genesis 1:26, Author's translation)

In verse 27, the phrase הָאָדָם (*Ha'Adom*) occurs for the first time:

"וַיִּבְרָא אֱלֹהִים אֶת־**הָאָדָם** בְּצַלְמוֹ בְּצֶלֶם אֱלֹהִים
בָּרָא אֹתוֹ זָכָר וּנְקֵבָה בָּרָא אֹתָם"

Va'yiv'ra Elohim et ***Ha'Adom*** *b'tzal'mo b'tze'lem Elohim bara oto za'char ou'n'kay'vah bara o'tom.*

"*Elohim* created ***Ha'Adom*** in His image. In the image of *Elohim*, He created him. Male and female He created them."

(Genesis 1:27, Author's translation)

Observe that **the maleness and the femaleness exist together** in the word *Adom* (אָדָם) (Genesis 1:26), but they are explicated and distinguished in the term הָאָדָם (*Ha'Adom*) (Genesis 1:27)!

Before the surgery in Genesis 2:21, the term *Adom* is used three times (Genesis 1:26; 2:5, and 2:20), while *Ha'Adom* is used ten times (Genesis 1:27; 2:7 (twice), 8, 15, 16, 18, 19 (twice), and 20). **After the surgery**, four pivotal events occur in Genesis 2:22–23: 1) both terms–*Adom* and *Ha'Adom*–are designated to the *maleness* of the human being; 2) the *femaleness* of the human being emerges; 3) the Hebrew term for the woman–**אִשָּׁה** (***Isha***)–appears for the first time; and 4) once *Isha* is built from *Ha'Adom*, *Ha'Adom* receives another name, **אִישׁ** (*Ish*). Look for the Hebrew terms **אִשָּׁה** and **אִישׁ** in Genesis 2:22–23:

> The Eternal-*Elohim* built up the side that He had taken from *Ha'Adom to the isha* (לְאִשָּׁה, *l'isha*) and he brought her to *Ha'Adom*. *Ha'Adom* said, "This time, [she is] bone of

> my bones and flesh of my flesh, to this she will be called *Isha* (אִשָּׁה, *Isha*) for she was taken from this" (Author's translation).

Commonly, when persons recount the creation of humanity, Adam and Eve are automatically identified, but the important historical and linguistic developments are ignored. Furthermore, "Eve" is not the woman's transliterated Hebrew name! Her Hebrew name is *Chavah* (חַוָּה), and she does not receive that designation until Genesis 3, after God **"built up the side that He had taken from *Ha'Adom*."** So, before Genesis 3, **only four terms** regarding humanity operate in the Hebrew text: *Adom*, *Ha'Adom*, *isha*, and *ish*.

In chapter 3 of Genesis, *isha* becomes *ha'Isha*. Interestingly, *ha'Ish* does **not occur** until Genesis 20. **In Genesis 3:20, *Ha'Adom* names his wife *Chavah***, which most English Bibles translate as Eve. In Genesis chapter 4, *Ha'Adom* intimately knows (*yada*) his wife *Chavah*, and she conceives two sons–*Kayin* (Cain) and *Hevel* (Able) (Genesis 4:1–2). In chapter 5, the term *Adom* is used **exclusively** in the first five verses without the definite Hebrew article "*ha*," which means "the." Below is a synopsis of Genesis 5:1–5.

1. *Adom* is created in the likeness of God. *Adom*'s progeny is chronicled. (v. 1)
2. *Elohim* created *Adom*. The verb בְּרָאָם (*b'ra'am*, He created them, Author's translation) signifies that *Elohim* created *Adom*. (v. 2)

3. God named the original human being, who was both *zachar* (male) and *n'kay'vah* (female), *Adom.* (v. 2)
4. *Adom* begets *Shet* (Seth) at the age of 130. (v. 3)
5. *Adom*'s lifespan after *Shet* is 800 years. (v. 4)
6. *Adom*'s total years on the earth are 930. (v. 5)

When you study the Hebrew text, notice how systematically God created and made humanity, male, and female. *Elohim*'s process was orderly and intricate. *Elohim* designed and distinguished maleness and femaleness "At the beginning."

The Transcription *Adonai* as a Substitute for The Tetragrammaton

I supplied a pronouncement for יְהוָה because Jews do not pronounce "יְהוָה"–God's sacred four-letter name. *In Your Sabbath Invitation*, I transcribed The Tetragrammaton as "*Yehovah*" one time to help the reader understand the material in chapter 10, "Freed from Temporary Life Support." Many Christians are probably more familiar with a transliteration of יְהוָה as YHWH or another variation of His name, rather than the term Tetragrammaton. When praying, Jews vocalize The Tetragrammaton as *Adonai* (LORD or Master), or they utter *HaShem* (The Name) when studying the Bible. When writing the four-letter name of God in an English biblical commentary, Jews will often write The Tetragrammaton as "YHWH," "YKVK," or as "Yud-Kay-Vav-Kay." Jews avoid vocalizing The Tetragrammaton to ensure that no one ever violates "taking the name of The Eternal in vain" (Exodus 20:7, Author's translation) or fails to adhere to "You should be in awe of The Eternal" (Deuteronomy 6:13, Author's translation).

The four-letter name יְהוָה is a fusion of "God will be (*yi'he'yeh*)," "God is (*ho'veh*)," and "God was (*ha'yah*)." Combined, the translation of The Tetragrammaton becomes "The Eternal," which means "God above time." One should remember that "The Eternal" is God's most personal name. According to Genesis 2:7, "The Eternal breathed life into the first human being" (Author's translation). In Exodus 34:6–7, after Moses had acquired the second tablets of the Ten Commandments (Ten Categorical Statements), God passes by Moses and proclaims, He is "…'The Eternal, The Eternal, compassionate and gracious God, slow to anger, abounding in lovingkindness and truth, extending lovingkindness to a thousand generations, who bears the iniquities, rebellion and sin, and absolving [the guilty who repent]…'" (Exodus 34:6–7a, Author's translation).